About the Author

Jack Freeman has led rather a dilettante life ranging from laundry delivery boy, RAF wireless operator, factory worker, employment advisor, musical street advertiser, professional rock guitarist, film extra in a Sting movie, mature literature student, product musical jingle producer, editor of a family history magazine and English language teacher. This involved travelling the world including hitch-hiking from Singapore to Bangkok and back. Some of his occupations led to radio and television appearances. He has retained a sense of humorous adventure tempered by common sense. He now is semi-retired and resides in Prague, teaching English and guitar and playing in local bands.

The Author at the Time

SWEATING ON MY CHITTY BOX

Jack Freeman

SWEATING ON MY CHITTY BOX

Vanguard Press

VANGUARD PAPERBACK

© Copyright **2024**
Jack Freeman

The right of Jack Freeman to be identified as author of this work has been asserted by him in accordance with the Copyright, Designs and Patents Act 1988.

All Rights Reserved

No reproduction, copy or transmission of this publication may be made without written permission.
No paragraph of this publication may be reproduced, copied or transmitted save with the written permission of the publisher, or in accordance with the provisions of the Copyright Act 1956 (as amended).

Any person who commits any unauthorised act in relation to this publication may be liable to criminal prosecution and civil claims for damages.

A CIP catalogue record for this title is available from the British Library.

ISBN 978 1 80016 680 6

*Vanguard Press is an imprint of
Pegasus Elliot Mackenzie Publishers Ltd.*
www.pegasuspublishers.com

First Published in **2024**

**Vanguard Press
Sheraton House Castle Park
Cambridge England**

Printed & Bound in Great Britain

Dedication

All the guys who were at El Adem from December 1961 to December 1963. And apologies for any names or facts I got wrong. (It was sixty years ago.)

My long-suffering family who have had to cope with my various schemes.

Acknowledgements

Steve Myers whose wonderful sketches brought it all back to life.

Lev Veshnyakov for processing the text and graphics and who, if alive at the time, would have been the enemy.

Chapter One
The Moving Finger Having Written

Having been allowed a year of grace stationed at various places in the UK after completing our eighteen-month training course, many of my original recruitment intake were simultaneously posted overseas. Gathered together again in the wilds of Gloucestershire for the purpose of embarkation and other bureaucratic machinations, we compared postings with varying degrees of dread directly related to each one's designated destination.

Like everyone else there I had been allowed three personal choices to be written out in order of preference. Again, like everyone there and in the same order, I had chosen Hong Kong, Singapore and Germany. Demonstrating that they too possessed a sense of humour, the haphazard map pricking members of the records department had allocated me for North Africa. Mysteriously many of the same people with whom I had shared a barrack room in training were also bound for the same place and, as it turned out, the same room.

After a week of idling around only partly occupied by making doorstep sandwiches for our more unfortunate companions who were chasing Ban the Bombers around the cold December countryside, we were all loaded onto a bus and driven to Gatwick airport to wait at the departure gate for Cunard Eagle who were contracted to fly RAF personnel. As most of us were young, not entirely innocent but nevertheless optimistic, it was a cheerful bunch that clattered up for our first encounter with the unknown and the customs. There had been tales of great hardship awaiting us at RAF El Adem.

"But no place with a romantic name like that could be bad. Could it? I mean it's near Tobruk and we've all heard of that place!"

Visions of Perspex be-goggled tank commanders making passes at scantily and diaphanously clad exotic women scorched through our constantly frustrated teenage souls. This pleasant mirage was broken by a drunken figure weaving its way to the departure terminal. It was an old man of at least twenty-eight. A veteran. And he was returning to El Adem after spending as riotous a time as possible on leave in good old Blighty. This was something we would all become very familiar with in the next two years of desert sojourn. He was bombarded with questions many bordering on the inane.

"What's El Adem like?"

"S'ell awlright!"

"Do the Arabs really cut your balls off for looking at their women?"

This last was received with a patronizing sneer and a further swig of his whisky bottle which fitted conveniently into his raincoat pocket. Some brave souls had allowed their parents to see them off and into their farewell embraces blundered our old sweat shouting, "What abaht me?" A warm-hearted woman, without a moment's hesitation, turned and kissed our bold drunken colleague. We all exchanged embarrassed but apprehensive glances. If this place drove people to such lengths for an embrace by a strange middle-aged female, its reputation may prove to be quite justified. On reflection I wish I had kissed her myself.

Even though we had all served at least three years to date, for most of us this was only our second flight. The first had been a fifteen-minute spin in an old Dakota — a token gesture by our employers to reassure us that we really were in the Royal Air Force with planes and everything. After hours of boredom only slightly relieved by the view of the hostess' inviting rear as she scurried past with the pilots' coffee ("No booze on this flight lads"), we circled what seemed to be a huge construction yard.

The gloomy scene presented what appeared to be partly demolished old buildings inter-spaced with tin huts presumably housing machinery. Despite our experiences so far, the air of expectant optimism was still present to a vague degree. It dispersed noticeably when we learned that the old disintegrating buildings were administration blocks and the little tin huts were our living quarters called Tynehams, probably the offspring of Nissen grown larger with a healthy post-war diet. Further disillusionment awaited.

Instead of the blazing sun and scorching sands inspired by Burt Lancaster gritting his famous grin and scrambling over the Californian beaches whilst wearing a French Foreign Legion outfit, we were greeted by a sea of mud, drizzling rain and temperatures only a little above the winter back home. This was December 1961 and, the Libyan setting notwithstanding, the Cold War could not have been any colder.

Once settled into one of the aforementioned huts we then started looking for something to do. As we were signallers we worked a shift system and this gave us plenty of free time. The usual military facilities of any camp were on offer such as the NAAFI canteen (Navy, Army and Air Force Institutes), a cinema and… and… and nothing. Communing with nature and fasting in the wilderness may be the perfect way for an Old Testament prophet to while away the odd month or two but, to a virile nineteen-year-old dying to become part of the new society soon to be called permissive, those delights were a little passé.

The commanding officer of the camp was well aware of these shortcomings and did his best to keep up the *esprit de corps*. Knowing the Lords of the Air would frown on something really constructive like importing plane loads of ladies of questionable virtue from the more disreputable areas of London's West End, he did the next best thing. He encouraged us to keep pets, (an unheard-of thing on any other military base), take up hobbies, sports or any other time-consuming scheme he could think up and for which he had quite a fund. The only alternative to these excitements was going to the pictures and then running down to the NAAFI before it closed to get stoned on conveniently cheap booze. En masse we went to the pictures and then ran down to the NAAFI and got stoned.

Chapter Two
A Christmas to Remember

One of the CO's inspirations that did not fall onto stony ground was the Christmas bar contest. The idea was that each department of the base, or even any loose organization of people so inclined, could build a bar and, on Christmas Day, the CO would visit each one, make as sober a judgement as possible, considering the circumstances, and award prizes to the best.

All serious activity stopped at about noon on Christmas Eve. The whole camp then began an orgy of drinking and wild horseplay that rivalled the little soirées Tiberius used to throw in Capri. Everyone staggered from bar to bar and, hardly pausing to admire the considerable ingenuity of each den's construction, they downed caseloads of Tennants lager, Watney's brown ale, and Johnny Walker whisky. All the beer came in cans but it was prior to the ring pull variety so each had to be opened by puncturing two holes in it with a metal device known irreverently as a church key. Thus, all conversation was punctuated by the stab of church keys and the hiss of escaping foam.

Leafy laden South Sea island bars, pirate taverns, an authentic British pub with highly varnished woodwork — each was imaginatively and creatively presented. A particularly original establishment was a caveman's bar. This was accessed by crawling through what appeared to be a tunnel that was hollowed out of stone. In reality, the walls were made of blankets specially treated to give the appearance and texture of solid rock. There was also a Western-style saloon complete with bat swing doors, an arrow-embedded mirror, roulette wheels and hundreds of town drunks. It fortunately did not run to ostrich be-feathered *females* in gaudy dresses as, in that celibate laden atmosphere, to have dressed up accordingly would have been too big a chance to take. The impressive thing about all of them was what each had been made from: a barrack room. Yet once inside it was impossible to imagine the usual drab surroundings of a billet with its similarity to a hospital ward. The most epic in scope and the inevitable winner was the Airfield Construction Squadron's bar.

A purple neon sign outside blinked on and off the words *Colosseum Bar*. Inside huge marble like pillars held up a ceiling illuminated with scenes of downtown Rome AD150. In the middle of the room was a fountain, in the centre of which was a statue of a naked dryad which poured water from a vase into the pool. The floor was completely covered in mosaic and, adding that little touch of authenticity, bearskin-clad slaves no doubt recently brought from Britannica lay snoring drunkenly in the corner, laden in chains.

Christmas Day dawned amidst an atmosphere of stale beer, vomit and urine. Stumbling from the places where they had fallen down the previous night, the inhabitants of El Adem poured straight back into or in some cases got off the floor of these bars and continued the marathon binge. At about noon an exodus began to the mess for Christmas dinner.

Traditionally served by the officers, this was initially conducted in a fairly civilized manner apart from a small amount of liberty taking permissible on such occasions. Then an impromptu singing session started up, heartily encouraged by our well-meaning CO. The padre too was particularly touched when we all sang *Swing Low Sweet Chariot*. This may seem a particularly unseasonal choice but this ditty is a forces' favourite. It is sung with soul searching fervour and accompanied by extremely lewd and suggestive gestures. The delighted grin of the poor padre became a little fixed after about the tenth chorus. He admired our enthusiasm but was a little doubtful about the sentiment. Having sung ourselves hoarse, the CO then gave out the prizes for the best bar. These consisted of our favourite currency: crates of beer. The climax came when the Airfield Construction Squadron on receiving their first prize padlocked the CO to the slaves and dragged him away in chains back to their palace of sin for further debauchery.

The rest of that day and Boxing Day passed by in a sort of haze, incidents from which are difficult to recall. I have vague memories of missing most of a free film show of *Oceans 11* (the original sixties Rat Pack version), losing an unsteady sword fight in one of the pirate taverns and ending up walking the plank fully clothed into a bath of water. But apart from those, no further details spring to mind.

Chapter Three
The Winter of our Discontent

After the Christmas celebrations, which had really been more reminiscent of the rites of an ancient Greek deity than a Christian festival, were over, life settled down to a routine of work, two different films a week on the cinema, and regular drinking sessions in the NAAFI. During winter these were the only entertainments available as, amongst hundreds of single men, there were approximately only six women. Two of whom were lesbians, three were over forty and the remaining one weighed sixteen stone.

Our frustrations were poured nightly into our sheets which came back from the laundry still stained. Which said a lot for the strength of British spunk but did not exactly inspire confidence in the efficiency of the laundry.

The camp had its own broadcasting system run by enthusiasts, the acronym title being ironically appropriate — T.EA.R.S. (Tobruk El Adem Radio Station). Like everything else on the base, the standard of presentation was fairly professional. This was due to the isolation. We had nothing to do most of the time so any activity was given wholehearted focus. As it was the early sixties, the British beat group scene was just gathering momentum albeit the Beatles had yet to raise their mop laden heads. So many hours were whiled away lying on our beds listening to the frenzied twangs and rebellious sounding vocals of the current hits. One night I particularly recall the speaker gushed out the syrupy sound of romantically played violins and, talking over these throbbing tones, oozed the most seductive female voice I have ever heard. She then proceeded to present a programme devoted entirely to songs of an extreme romantic nature which had been requested by girlfriends and wives back home.

Not content with merely saying who the songs were for and from whom, this alluring voice in an orgy of exquisite sadism breathed tormenting sentiments like "Peter Gunton of Twneham 21 do you remember that star-kissed night beneath the old pier at Liverpool when Connie, your own sweet Connie whose perfume made your senses reel, was in your arms?"

After ten minutes of this mildly pornographic torture, I ran out of the hut and got heartily drunk in the NAAFI. But not withstanding my curiosity was aroused. Who was this silken voiced siren who risked an invasion of the radio hut by sex crazed teenage airmen?

The next day all was revealed. Strolling out of the mess mug of tea in hand I was brought up short. Standing with her back to me was what appeared to be a blue clad female hippopotamus. Gargantuan buttocks of awesome proportions were bent over whilst their owner was installing budgerigars and canaries into a miniature aviary at the entrance to the mess hall. As I drew level, this human brontosaurus talked and clucked to her little feathered charges and out of that massive frame poured that orgasm-inducing voice. It was our new mess officer. Ashen faced, I stumbled to work with a deep sense of having been cheated somehow even later unsuccessfully attempting to teach the budgies obscenities. The woman's appearance not matching her promising voice was just one of those things, but to this day whenever I hear the saccharine sound of

Mantovani's Orchestra an involuntary shudder will shake my frame in a loathsomely nostalgic quiver.

Chapter Four
The Garden

As the weather grew warmer and the flies increased in numbers and the days crawled past in mind dulling stifling heat, a further attempt to alleviate the interminable boredom was made by our public-spirited CO. There we all were, in the middle of the largest desert area in the world, and the CO's mind was on cultivation. What we all needed was a touch of greenery and, with unquenchable optimism, he organized a gardening contest.

I was in my usual prone position on my bed reading *Dr No* by Ian Fleming and idly pondering that James Bond would make a successful film character when the great news was broken to me. Infected by the CO's enthusiasm my fellow inmates had caught gardening fever.

"Come on, get off your arse, you lazy little bastard," and similar inducements were offered to make me assist their agricultural endeavours. But, knowing that the view outside was three hundred and sixty degrees of flat horizon broken only by the occasional shrub — a view guaranteed to make Alan Titchmarsh throw in his trowel, I was unable to match their cultivating zeal. With threats that if they won the five-pound prize I would receive no share they started digging tons of sandy soil. Thinking that a fiver amongst eight people did not exactly rival Paul Getty's little nest egg, I returned to the exciting adventures of double o seven.

Apart from the occupation therapy angle, these horticultural dreams of the CO did have some scientific basis. He had studied Libya's history and informed us that this had been the principal wheat growing country of the Roman Empire and, what's more, the soil had been analysed and only needed watering to prove abundantly fertile. What he had not considered was the vast manpower resources in slaves that empire possessed plus the fact that all our water, apart from that treated for drinking, was called saline and had a high salt content. An ingredient which did not exactly encourage growth in a freshly planted begonia.

Despite these difficulties, the budding sharecroppers laboured on. Little walls of cement were erected with ten-centimetre gaps in between and they transferred the dry soil from outside the walls into the gaps between and optimistically planted seeds to brave the onslaught of the merciless sun. In their frenzied efforts to enhance the African countryside, they found a small miracle. It was a twenty-centimetre square of grass which they carefully dug up intact and transplanted to a specially built plinth immediately outside our tin hut's verandah.

The day of judgement finally arrived and the CO's Land Rover pulled up outside. At his first glimpse of our rolling turf, his face lit up. It was the clincher. They won the contest by a mile. Visitors to our desert paradise were driven down to our billet to view the phenomenon of possibly the only patch of genuine grass for a thousand miles. Many was the time I would be hanging out my Y fronts on the hut's washing line to be greeted by the CO in the company of some bemused air traveller pointing excitedly to our lawn.

"Don't forget to water it," he would plead.

"Oh no, sir, we always remember," we truthfully replied. Which we did every night on returning from the NAAFI, the latrines being situated some distance away. Yes, I was very proud of the garden that I did not help to build.

Chapter Five
The Siege of the NAAFI Roof

The conditions led to us living in each other's pockets and gave us the opportunity of observing first hand each person's developing eccentricities engendered by the nature of our mutual predicament. I believe that these were sanity preserving techniques because of our circumstances rather than the symptoms of mental aberration caused by them. In other words, we all acted mad to stay sane. Each one of us gained some new habit that had never been apparent before in our two-year association with each other. Some of these traits would be extremely irritating and also tended to grow out of all proportion to the thing itself. This could sometimes lead to heated arguments, but these idiosyncrasies were mainly tolerated and became part of life's rich pasture. Our experience was comparable to the months that sailors spend away from home at sea. The only difference being we never docked at the more exotic ports of the world but were becalmed near Tobruk which makes a small UK fishing village seem like the burgeoning wharf area of San Francisco.

Bryn Hughes would fall asleep with his eyes open. This was particularly disconcerting when, after a long sentence during a conversation, you addressed a question to him, only to realize on receiving a light snore in reply that he had been asleep for some time. In retrospect it is remarkable that my own personal habit, considering the form it took, was tolerated and never complained about and demonstrated the depth of tolerance shared by my companions. In the middle of the night, in that half-conscious state between being awake or asleep my frustrated brain with waves of self-pitying thoughts breaking against the blank wall of the utter helplessness of my situation, I would pound the side of my small wardrobe in noisy impotent fury. Time is relative and the older I get the faster it seems to go. But in those turbulent teenage years, a fairly active week was a long time so months of enforced idleness seemed like centuries and heightened to extremes by the situation. Peter Flattery and Andy Legge's quirks were not so obvious but really more disturbing. Both of these characters behaved, to be ambiguous, too normally.

Pete, who was obviously going far in the promotion stakes, was a paragon of virtue. His efficiency at work was highly impressive and matched his immaculate appearance. The only vice he acquired was a constant flow of neatly written letters to his fiancée back home — a habit he indulged in daily. Andy Legge, surrounded by large blow-up shots of his beautiful girlfriend, would duplicate Pete's behaviour only breaking off to fiddle with his marquetry set, a hobby he became highly skilled at. I retain every respect for these two people but sometimes wonder what dark thoughts were harboured beneath those unassuming exteriors, and luckily kept successfully in check by what must have been iron wills and in the face of the remainder's extrovert behaviour was doubly impressive. One of the more colourful occupants of the hut was a Welshman, Ted Evans, who was inevitably called Taff as are all natives of that country who are members of Her Majesty's forces.

Although of only some five feet two inches in height he became the billet's champion drinker indulging in quaffing sessions of legendary proportions. This was some achievement as even I, with no real reputation for drink, often used to have a beer before I got out of bed in the morning. Taff's most memorable adventure was The Siege of the NAAFI Roof. For full appreciation of this tale a certain amount of background detail is necessary.

Each evening the bar in the NAAFI closed at ten, stemming the flow of brain numbing alcohol and allowing the exhausted staff time to lick the wounds inflicted whilst serving a queue that started at opening time and tried frantically to push the descending shutters back up at closing time. The far sighted would buy a stock of beer before then, usually in the form of a crate for each person (twenty-four cans) and then sit around the tables in the patio of the NAAFI and complacently drink it. Needless to say, Ted belonged to this fraternity of moonlight drinkers. These little affairs would go on for an hour after closing until dispersed by the authorities. It was the unfortunate task of the orderly corporal (who could have been one of the revellers himself on previous occasions) to start the initial pleas to move.

These exhortations were usually ignored by the jovial crowd, in fact the noise was such that I doubt they even heard. If the case was pursued too closely threats of a violent nature were usually enough to discourage any further attempts and the luckless NCO would retire in defeat to enlist the aid of the orderly sergeant. The whole rigmarole would then be repeated until, in desperation, the RAF Police would be called out. Crowds of jeering drunks would then be pursued by the police Land Rover.

They would run around the barrack blocks laughing hysterically and obviously enjoying the chase. I suspect the police enjoyed it too as it must have broken the monotonous patrol for native pilferers whom they never succeeded in apprehending.

On the night in question, Taff had become bored with just sitting drinking and had climbed onto the NAAFI roof accompanied by the inevitable crate of Amstel beer. When this too began to pall, he enlivened the proceedings by hurling empty cans at those below. They of course returned them. Soon the place was a battleground. Those combatants on the ground were throwing cans up at Taff; he was frantically drinking his crate to replenish the ammunition, (the idea of using a full can being dismissed not for safety reasons but for the sacrilegious reason of the waste). Due to his tactical advantage,

Taff was gamely holding his own when an aluminium garden chair thrown with deadly accuracy knocked him off the roof. At that precise moment the orderly corporal was just coming around the corner having nerved himself up for the futile clearing procedure previously described. A small figure landed

on the concrete immediately in front of his startled gaze with a damp thud. Transfixed with the horror of what appeared to be a fatal accident, the corporal was rooted to the spot. Ted, meanwhile, groaned sat up and said, "Where's me crate? Ah! There it is." He picked up his beer which he had manfully kept hold of during his short flight and walked home where he and I finished off the crate on my bed as he recounted the tale of that evening's activities.

Another of Taff's accomplishments was an ability to break wind practically non-stop. He would use this talent to punctuate conversations, express disgust or to emphasize a point. During one such musical sounding debate, the subject of breaking wind itself was brought up. Various styles were discussed — Ted reckoning his own personal high-pitched form being due to an extremely neat and tight anal aperture and, therefore, superior to those strong-smelling silent ones that must emerge from huge flabby backsides. We were exploring the various degrees of odorous intensity when someone said, "'ere Taff did you know that farts are supposed to be inflammable?"

The die was cast. Without further ado Ted removed his clothing, lit up his Ronson cigarette lighter, held it at the appropriate angle and lustily broke wind. Immediately his lower limbs and torso were enveloped in flames. Taff, hardy soul that he was, never uttered a sound. He just lay there looking at his crisply charred pubic hair. Meanwhile the rest of us were collapsed on our beds prostrate with joyous glee. From then on, in moments of stress, Ted would lift up his towel and our flagging spirits and stage his own pyrotechnic show. This being doubly appreciated at night with the lights off.

Chapter Six
Guardians of the Empire

Each of us had to take a turn at guard duty and my first stint at this proved to be quite a baptism of fire.

A little hut housing bunk beds was situated at the side entrance we were to guard and the four unfortunates on duty took turns to sleep. The idea was to stop all traffic, pedestrian or otherwise, that approached the said gate, which for some reason was always left open at night. How we were to stem the invading hordes of Egyptian soldiery armed only a with a telephone I find it hard to imagine but that was supposed to be our function.

During my turn I baulked at standing outside in the cold but settled down by the paraffin stove and lost myself in the latest saga of Mickey Spillane (my literary taste at the time did not yet include the joys of E.M Forster or Solzhenitsyn). Immersed in a world of terse grim men who dodged bullets whilst making casual passes at dangerous looking redheads, I was dimly aware of an approaching motor.

Thinking with a false sense of security that, as it was approaching from inside the camp it posed no threat, I ignored it. The next moment the door crashed open and an angry RAF policeman (quaintly and ironically named Snowdrops after the winter flower due to their white hats) complete with holstered gun, confronted my startled gaze, and with flames leaping out of his eyes he demanded who was supposed to be on guard. His face already red with dutiful anger deepened visibly as I confessed to be the current one. Ignoring my reasonable explanations about vehicle direction, no weaponry etc., he berated my lack of vigilance with a vehemence terrible to suffer. Knowing that a charge with its punishment of confinement to barracks held little fear in our particular environment he used that cliché penalty beloved of military policemen the world over.

"And get yer 'air cut first thing tomorrow and report to me at the guardroom to see it."

The Rolling Stones were yet to flaunt their long locks at the world but hair loomed very large in our legend. Hours were spent patiently training our quiff hairstyles. My own had just reached a satisfactory sweeping luxuriant splendour, so it was a reluctant rock and roller who sat and watched the barber reap his grim harvest the following day. I presented myself for inspection at the guard house.

"Call that a bleedin' 'aircut? I'm standing on it you should be in pain!" (The Snowdrop was no lover of originality.)

"Get back and get it done properly."

Seething with indignant martyrdom I returned to the barber shop and requested further shearing and once more returned to the guardroom. To my utter disbelief I was once more ordered back to the barber's. Ablaze with anger I returned and this time told the incredulous Libyan barber to shave it all off. But he, having some sympathy for my cause by now, persuaded otherwise and cut my hair in a semi-crewcut style which is now called a flat top I believe — even refusing further payment for his services. This last session appeased my tormentors — well it had to really there was little left to remove but it left its mark. During my two-year tour of duty at El Adem and on every base I was stationed thereafter, I managed to establish a record of haircut avoidance second to none. Glorying in the fact that when on leave I was never believed to be a serviceman but only another example of a typical teenage layabout who could do with a stint of National Service (outmoded mandatory military service always revered as a cure for teenage rebellion) to sort me out.

Chapter Seven
The Silver Screen

Although it had to suffer the unimaginative name of the Astra (I never came across an RAF cinema not called that) the cinema was second only to masturbation and boozing as the most popular form of escapism. It used to present two shows each evening. Although the films themselves only changed twice a week each house was packed with sweating, swearing airmen. Possibly thinking that in the strained circumstances our patriotic fervour was a little low, the powers that be in their wisdom showed a film of the Queen and played the national anthem at the beginning of the performance instead of at the end as usual in most cinemas at that time. Once the chorus of catcalls, boos, hisses and colourful expletives along with the odd thrown empty soft drinks bottle had died down, the show commenced.

Cartoons were really big. A roar of approval greeting the opening music. The names on the credits were shouted out with hearty enthusiasm and even today whilst watching Tom and Jerry on television I have a tendency to scream, "Good old Fred", when the name of Fred Quimby the producer appears. No film was too high or low brow for our Catholic tastes, because, if a piece of celluloid proved to be a little slow, it would be enlivened by spontaneous advice from the stalls.

"G'wan rip her knickers off! Get stuck in there!"

These sages would cry to a broken Clark Gable as he held a weeping Marilyn Monroe in *The Misfits*.

Approving applause would greet any extreme anti-social behaviour portrayed. The loudest I witnessed was when the main protagonist in *A Kind of Loving* threw up all over his mother-in-law's carpet.

Another function of the cinema was to feature the travelling C.S.E. (Combined Services Entertainment) shows that toured those British bases still clinging dogmatically to the more remote corners of the globe. Many well-known stars of the time would grace the modest little stage. Harry Secombe, David Whitfield, Edna Savage and the Allisons who came second in the 1961 Eurovision song contest all appeared at our Astra. All of these entertainers were given a wonderful reception. Like servicemen in bleak situations all over the world, we may have not been in a war but our Beau Geste scenario had that other oft mentioned aspect of more war-like military biographies — months of incredible boredom. So starved of live entertainment and also pining to be free we were doubly appreciative.

At that time one performer on tour was Yana a woman whose main talent was the size of her bosom.

The evening she performed, the camp outside was a ghost town. One could even be served easily at the

NAAFI bar as there was no ten-person queue. The curtain went up and there she stood in all her overdeveloped glory. The crowd reached new heights of imaginative response as, her well-rounded frame swaying enticingly, she began to sing somewhat uninspiringly. However, this was a mere detail to the voracious mob of ravenous men. The noise receded slightly as the crowd noticed a hulking figure rise up from its seat at the far side of the room and shamble purposefully down the side aisle.

Unaware of this approaching menace and probably thinking the lower volume meant her vocal talents were finally being appreciated as much as her other gifts, Yana continued emoting.

This stumbling figure belonged to Steve Dawson a man of a considerable and much valued reputation. He was the camp drunk and amongst that crowd of devoted drinkers this was no mean feat. Noted for never being sober on or off duty or uttering a sentence when one word or a grunt would suffice, Corporal Steve Dawson drifted through our small world in a permanent alcoholic haze. Some deep rooted and primeval instinct must have been stirred by the panorama of Yana's enticing flesh. But who knows what emotions flared beneath that massive stomach? He ascended the stage from the wings and Yana sang on oblivious, singing a song that pleaded, "Take me I'm yours".

Two huge hairy arms plucked her up away from the microphone and turned her around and muffled her initial and frightened scream with a long passionate kiss. She was then deposited in a rather breathless condition back on the stage and Steve, having not said one word, lurched back down the stairs and returned to his seat. Recovering herself and once the ecstatic howl at Steve's antics had diminished, she asked, "Who was that big bear?" For the remainder of his tour of duty at El Adem and possibly his whole RAF career, Corporal Steve Dawson, Telegraphist One, was known as Yogi.

Chapter Eight
Zoological Studies

Until I was stationed at El Adem animals, apart from normal boyhood pets, had played only a small part of life and were not allowed on RAF camps anyway. But under the benign gaze of our CO, the keeping of pets was not only allowed but actively encouraged. The local animals were mainly a sort of mangy yellow coloured dog referred to as Pye, some cats and, one of the most popular, the incredible chameleon lizard.

The latter were highly prized. Not only because of their entertaining way of changing colour or hissing nastily when teased, but for the more practical reason that they killed and ate our biggest enemies: flies. Forget snakes, scorpions or poisonous spiders, the common house fly was second only to boredom of the hardships we endured. I was one of the proud owners of these primordial beauties whom I named Fred after a winsome redhead back home who was christened Freda Brown. Many a happy hour was passed by feeding Fred because it fulfilled two functions. Firstly there was the fascination of watching the lizard's method of killing and eating his prey, and secondly, the satisfaction of knowing that by however small an amount the fly population was being steadily depleted. Fred would be lying on the back of my hand and I would point him, or her (gender was never established), like some reptilian pistol at some unsuspecting fly. Its whole body would then freeze into instant immobility. The pink tip of its tongue would emerge and then 'Kapow' with deadly accuracy his long sticky tongue would lash out and recoil with the hapless fly. Fred was always being lost, not because of any great desire to escape, but his ability to change colour and match his surroundings made him practically invisible. Once after a particularly long search he was found clinging to my record rack wearing a pure white skin, that being the colour of the back of the Elvis Presley album *King Creole* he was beside.

Apart from not being able to fully satisfy our more carnal desires, the lack of female companionship starved us all of an outlet for our more affectionate emotions. Lavishing attention on the local fauna went a long way to assuage these feelings. Animals who would normally have had the most precarious sort of existence were cared for to the point of ridiculousness. A procession of men bearing plates of the gristle-laden meat so beloved by our catering staff would wend its way from the mess after every meal time. The animals would all gather around as there was never any distinction because everyone fed everybody's pets. Sometimes, whilst having a late bath, I would be interrupted by what appeared to be the cries of a maternity nursery, only to realize they were the mating yowls of our resident cat population, bent on expansion.

A particularly vicious member of the canine species, aptly named Brutus, lived in one of the huts near ours. He was continually chasing the odd Erk (non-commissioned airman) who, in Brutus' opinion, had infringed on his territory. Consequently, his owners enjoyed a freedom from intruders unrivalled on the camp. Tales of his successful encounters with other animals, people and Land Rovers were legend and recounted amidst wild hilarity in the NAAFI (as has already been pointed out we were starved for entertainment). One evening, his completely misnamed brother Geronimo, a dog of a very docile nature, was being encouraged by the regulars in the bar to complete his sex education under the tutelage of a willing bitch in season who was also in the bar. No amount of cajolery or threats could induce the shy Geronimo to mount his eager companion. The crowd were being quite generous really, thinking that just because they were deprived of an active sex life there was no reason why Geronimo should suffer too. They thought he was being ungrateful and did not know when he was well off. Into this licentious scene appeared Brutus. Chairs and tables were scattered in a tangle of spilt beer and broken glassware as people hastily removed themselves from Brutus' flashing fangs as his reputation by then was firmly established. A terse snarl reduced his brother's reluctant passion to the point of his running out the door and Brutus then fulfilled the role his brother had been so reluctant to play right under the outraged gaze our NAAFI's female manager.

Alas poor Brutus was living on borrowed time. One day he went too far and committed the cardinal sin. He bit an RAF policeman. Every one of us knew how he felt as we all had to curb similar urges every other day. He was carted off by the Snowdrops and put down. One of his owners was Bill Davison the drunk we had met at Gatwick airport. When sober he had an ironic sense of the poetic. After telling the sad story of Brutus' incarceration and subsequent execution, he sighed and slightly misquoting said, "Ah well. Them that lives by the sword dies by the sword. Et tu Brutus."

In the main our insect life fell short of true entertainment, more a healthy respect as most of its representatives were equipped with a nasty bite. Apart from squadrons of house flies there was another winged foe with heavier armament.

"Camel fly!"

The cry would go up and all would hurriedly duck as the confident pilot cruised through the air space of our tin home. The equivalent of a horse fly, this tough character was impossible to swat. Even if one settled on a wall and was clouted with a boot there was every chance of it only becoming enraged rather than fatally injured and as a result would chase its would-be assassin around the room. The only known way to dispatch this insect Gorbals dweller (a then very tough district in

Glasgow) was to trap it between the wall and the sole of a flip flop, lean your full weight on the firmly held sandal and scrape it along the wall. Even this method was not a certainty; the usual ploy adopted was to open a hopeful window and lie low.

Scorpions both black and khaki invaded our domain, waddling across the floor with threatening tails but a long-handled broom would soon kill one of these, although for a few days after its demise we would check the inside of our footwear but then revert back to the normal indifferent hungover sleepy search with extended foot. Not so easy to immobilize was the camel spider, (the namer of these insects must have suffered from a lack of imagination or possibly bore a grudge against the famous desert steamer as it seemed to be used to name a lot of unpleasant creatures). If the scorpion was the tank, then the camel spider was the armoured car because its turn of speed was very impressive. Including its legs, this spider covered an equivalent area to a large soup bowl. Feet would be hastily lifted onto cots when one appeared running speedily but sideways along the bare boards of our dusty dormitory. (Oh yes we had it rough all right!) A more harmless intruder was the dung beetle. These large industrious dung rollers would often be observed making their laborious way across the hut in a hopeful but futile hunt for dung. Our habits were pretty bad but it was too optimistic of the beetles to think they could find any in our room.

Idly watching one such toiler one day, Taff Evans gave into a sadistic whim. Using his knowledge of practical engineering he constructed a *Dung Beetle Extermination Machine.* This was in the form of a cardboard box, inside which he had laid two lines of wire that formed a loop. These wires were then connected to an electrical plug. He then collected a half dozen of these luckless creatures and put them into the box and then connected the contraption to the mains. He waited until an unsuspecting beetle trod on the wire and then threw the main switch. The beetle would spasm as the power hit it and then lie still when Ted turned it off. Once he had, "Sent all of them to the chair" he lost interest, put the plug back on my record player and threw the box with its unfortunate contents outside. Later on, passing this coffin on my way to the showers in utter disbelief I watched a beetle crawl out from under it and bumble away across the sandy ground. It must have taken the biggest surge because on lifting the box I saw that all the rest must have already recovered and had disappeared, an ability the inhabitants of Alcatraz's death row would have loved to have shared.

Bryn Hughes's sister was a student and in her letters to him expressed a desire to possess some specimens from Libya. Having held a secret crush for her since introduced as a callow youth of sixteen, I became rather adept at catching scorpions and spiders with a broom and shovel. Regrettably I had no means of killing them without smashing their bodies so I stored them in a cardboard box whilst I pondered this problem. They solved it for me by killing each other in mortal conflict which we watched like so many attenders of the contests of Ancient Rome none of us having the nerve to break up the gladiators. However, this venture into entomology did not further my unvoiced passion for Bryn's sister.

Above each of our beds hung a mosquito net which were mainly used to escape the ceaseless attentions of the flies, as mosquitoes were relatively rare. However, this green stranded shroud proved to be no barrier to the bed bug. This miniature Dracula would crawl stealthily like a diminutive Christopher Lee into our bedclothes probably using the net as a ladder. Even as I write this my skin crawls with the memory of their bloodthirsty attentions. They seemed to thrive on the gallons of insecticide poured into the floor. I suspect they migrated to the ceiling supports the moment their radar sensed the approach of the extermination truck then crawled back down knowing that the holy water from the truck had evaporated. Once, I woke up, and was unable to fully open my eyes because they had bitten my eyelids which had swollen so much I could not prise them apart.

Although not too afraid of creepy crawlies there is one nemesis I share with a large proportion of anthropoids and that is an inbuilt fear of poisonous snakes. I find it hard to relate these sinewy reptiles to some 'vast eternal plan' and when wandering over the sand they were never far away from my thoughts. One morning on the way to work I was passing the transit buildings that were adjacent to the air terminal when I heard a noise directly in front of me. It was a similar sound to a bicycle tyre being rolled over sandy ground. I froze. Slithering towards a nearby bird at a tremendous rate was a thin sandy coloured snake that had just vacated the spot my bare leg would have trodden on in the next split second. For some reason known only to my belated self-preservation instinct I jumped over this spot, turning in mid-air to face the direction I had come from. Shaking off a peculiar paralysing sensation I walked towards the transit block whose temporary occupants were wandering about in flip-flops. I warned them about the proximity of the snake which was now prowling around the terrain near their rooms no doubt building up hopes of a handy leg to bite, his bird hunt having failed. We joined forces and, unlike the self-righteous crowds who corrected erring women in the New Testament, threw stones at the snake having no qualms about our various sins. The snake was cornered by the wall of the hut and gamely reared up and lashed at the missiles, but on meeting rock instead of nice teeth-yielding flesh, it gave up and with a noise like a cracking whip disappeared under the hut. I fully understood the transients' reluctance to leave it just like that. They did have to sleep there. We enlisted the aid of a nearby native Libyan who obviously thought we were making a fuss about nothing. Openly laughing at our faint-heartedness he thrust his hand under the hut and felt around unconcernedly. When you read these phrases they become clichés, but my heart was in my mouth as I watched this courageous, but in my opinion crazy, action.

"No snake there, John."

He grinned, dusted his hand on his old army greatcoat and walked off. I tottered into work and told the tale of my latest brush with death. From my description it was established that I had nearly trodden on an asp. I would love to have been crushed to Cleopatra's bosom but would not have been willing to share the experience with one of them.

Of all the sections of our close-knit society the cooks were amongst the least popular. This was an unusual prejudice as on most camps the friendship of these culinary gentlemen was highly prized for obvious reasons. A combination of causes may have led to this. First of all, the food was really bad. To be fair the fault was partly due to the huge transport problems and a reliance on such commodities as powdered potato, powdered egg and tinned preserves. But apart from this, the particular clique of cooks stationed with us had formed a sort of gang with overtones of the melodrama of such films as *Rebel Without A Cause* or *West Side Story*. Clad, even when off duty, in their blue and white checked trousers held up by a belt with a multiple sheath containing butcher knives plus a long cylindrical sharpener, they swaggered about the camp. None of us were particularly frightened or awed by this behaviour, more baffled. Who were they trying to impress? Determined to attract as much attention as possible these sad characters gave each other Huron hairstyles literally forming their own tribe. Their antics were greeted with derisive laughter but things became more serious and a rather distasteful symptom surfaced.

All of us who were off duty were ordered to present ourselves at the mess one day to be addressed by our CO. We all dutifully appeared anticipating one of the

CO's mad schemes to be announced. Do not be misled by any derisive description so far because the CO was the most popular figure in the camp. We all loved him dearly as he had that unusual quality amongst officers — an ability to come across as a human being without the usual patronising superiority of his breed. His boyish face set in a stern expression he told us all that a completely skinned dead cat had been found. The eyes of all glared at our resident tribe of Hurons who would return no one's gaze. We all knew what kind of headgear was favoured by the North American woodsmen such as Davy Crocket. He then elaborated saying that apart from the bestial act itself what, or rather who, would be next? There was no other evidence apart from the corpse itself so he concluded by urging us all to practice extreme caution and inform the authorities of any further such incidents. Needless to say, there were no more such happenings. The cooks' fashion of walking around armed to the teeth went out of style and their scalp-locks shaved off.

There it was only 1962 and they had already pioneered two later hairstyles: skinhead and punk.

Chapter Nine
Now it Can be Told

Most events of interest occurred off duty because, in spite of our rather eccentric general behaviour, at work we were all very efficient. This again was due to the isolated conditions. Work, because it passed the time, got our undivided attention. Aircraft with a minor fault would limp onto our base, the pilots refusing earlier attention knowing they would receive servicing of a speed and quality unmatched elsewhere. My own particular forte as a signaller was practiced in shifts around a twenty-four-hour day.

Radio operating using Morse code was an aspect of our trade rarely used in Britain, the main method being teleprinters but, due to atmospheric conditions, El Adem used a great deal of wireless telegraphy which by then was considered a little archaic. New arrivals were, therefore, often not well practiced in this skill but in a short while became as competent as the rest. This system did have more appeal than the impersonal chattering of a teleprinter because every wireless operator when using a Morse key has an individual style which creates a sense of actually talking to someone.

Our counterparts in Malta were civilians whose abilities were phenomenal and demonstrated a speed and accuracy of awesome proportions. Legend had it that these gentlemen were paid by the amount of work they produced which accounted for the speed they sent messages at. This seems doubtful now but whether it was due to their Latin temperament or this alleged assumption is debatable but their impatience with new arrivals was a standing joke. Sometimes they would be so incensed by the slow receiving and erratic transmissions of newcomers they would make insulting remarks like, "English pig". This of course only annoyed the Scots, Irish and Welsh amongst us. One such enraged Celt ripped his receiver off the bench and hurled it out of the signals cabin onto the rocky ground outside in frustrated fury. This precarious relationship became the hallmark of an individual's ability. The day you communicated with Malta without upsetting the operator you had arrived.

One evening an eerie reminder of the past happened. Bryn Hughes, to add colour and excitement to a dull existence, had volunteered to be radio operator for the Desert Rescue Service crew. These daring souls, having first of all loaded their vehicles with as much beer as possible, would set off into the Sahara on manoeuvres and practice runs lasting days at a time. They would stop at regular intervals to send routine messages of location at prearranged times. This particular evening the familiar routine was changed. In their more or less aimless wanderings they had come across the wreck of a USA bomber that had lain undiscovered since World War II. This was the remains of the *Lady Be Good,* a Liberator bomber that crashed in the desert. The official story is that this plane was found by a team of BP workers. However, I was on duty when this discovery was announced and believe that it was the Desert Rescue who first discovered this stark reminder of days gone by.

They also found the remains of the crew and again this conflicts with the official story, but whatever the truth is, it is a sobering thought that the next of kin of those long dead boys would be informed and they would have to relive the tragedy that had happened nearly twenty years before. Interestingly, a seventies movie was made inspired by this incident starring William Shatner of *Star Trek* fame and Richard Basehart which featured the discovery of a bomber in the desert which was still being watched over by its crew who were ghosts and were earth bound. The unfolding story revealed the reason for this which involved the only survivor, the navigator, who had bailed out over the Mediterranean.

Lighter moments did of course brighten up some of the working shifts. There was the day the Russians landed. This unlikely event occurred very close to the Cuban crisis which has no bearing on this tale except for the mistaken and fearful conclusion it precipitated in myself. Making my reluctant way to work one hot afternoon (not that there were many cold ones) I approached the wireless cabin which was on the ground floor of the Air Traffic Control tower. As I neared the marshalling area for planes known to us as the Pan I was exposed to a sight that made the adrenalin roar into my veins. There on the pan was an unfamiliar looking blue aircraft sporting a single stark crimson star. As my terrified gaze refocused itself and travelled on it picked out another one, two, three, four, five Russian MIG fighters boldly strutting on Her Royal Majesty's leased Libyan turf. Frantically my dazed brain ran through the options. To the west was Algeria and we were not all that friendly with them. To the east Egypt — and at that time our relations with that country were distinctly uncordial. Ahead was the Mediterranean Sea and behind me stretched the impassable wastes of the Sahara desert with a survival time measured in hours. In which direction should I flee?

El Adem's main function was as a petrol station for the machines flying the airborne motorway to and from the Far East. Our defences were non-existent — the words flack and ack ack were outmoded phrases more familiar to our parents than our Swinging Sixties selves. As noted earlier we even guarded things with only telephones as weapons. The only aircraft available to us was an unarmed Provost, a light plane capable of carrying eight or so passengers. Views of hundreds of frantic escapees clinging to the wings and tail fin whipped through my fear crazed brain. This whirl of panicking and frankly disloyal thoughts was suddenly brought to a sheepish halt. A group of camera enthusiasts and plane spotters were crowded around the invading MIGs excitedly taking photographs. Realizing that Nikita Krushchev's boys would not behave with such tolerance when engaged in freeing the workers from capitalism's ugly face my fear subsided and was replaced by curiosity. I continued to work to ask questions.

An hour or so earlier our control tower was called up by one of the MIGs and asked for permission to land because of engine trouble. This plane was part of a consignment that had been given to Egypt by Russia. They were of obsolete design and the Egyptians were generously donating them to the Algerians. This was a British military base so the control tower refused permission but the pilot took no notice and landed anyway, closely followed by his colleagues who must have thought he needed the moral support. The moment the planes taxied onto the pan the occupants, amidst much military ballyhoo, were taken into custody and the machines impounded. The pilots were of various nationalities neither of which was Egyptian, Algerian or Russian but one was British. Sometime later, after negotiations the details of which I remain in ignorance, a service aircraft with the necessary part arrived and the planes were allowed to continue their journey the next day. The nuclear holocaust had been avoided. An incongruous side issue of this was the confiscation of the poor shutterbug's films. There seemed no security reason for this as the planes were not on our secret list, belonged to the enemy and were obsolete anyway. I suspect it was a case of unwanted publicity. It would not enhance the image of an ever-vigilant nuclear wielding modern air force if naughty Egyptian fighters could drop in for tea whenever they felt like it. A further irony is that the Egyptians did eventually attack El Adem in the seventies, by then under Libyan management.

Chapter Ten
The Prime of Leonard Thomas

Most of my roommates had been acquainted with each other since they were sixteen having been trained together as Boy Entrants or *Brats* as we were more popularly known. An exception to this was Tom. Leonard Thomas was a West Indian from Antigua whose sunny disposition matched his home climate. He and I became firm friends, having many interests in common especially music. Like all new arrivals or *Moonies* (this term applied to the degree of suntan acquired and not to any religious organisation — though in Tom's case it was superfluous anyway), Tom did not really believe the limitations put on our social life at El Adem. After a short tour of the facilities on offer he still insisted that there must be more. A great lover of the opposite sex whilst in more populated surroundings he was still disbelieving of the arid years ahead.

"How about this joint Tobruk man? Let's go paint the town red!" was his enthusiastic cry.

Shrugging sardonically, I agreed to accompany him to this most famous of Eastern metropolae.

The desert as it approaches the coast suddenly drops hundreds of metres. A spiralling road similar to a helter-skelter corkscrews its dangerous way from the plateau and levelling off enters Tobruk.

My first sight of the town when I too had been as hopeful as Tom a million years or two months prior, was my own final moment of disillusionment. As the bus turned the corner into the town the crumbling walls of the building ahead displayed a series of small holes. I realized they were bullet holes probably fired by a tank's machine gun as it rounded the bend and attacked the town. A grim reminder of the town's wartime role. That of course was its only claim to fame. Looking as though the Germans had just vacated the premises to give the Australians their turn of occupation the town stood frozen in the time of twenty years before. Making the town look like the landscape's blot it was, the beautiful Mediterranean Sea of a blue to gladden any poet's eye swelled and broke onto gleaming beaches. This was the only reason to visit the place. Swimming in its warm waters during the eight months of summer became one of my most pleasant memories and has left me with little enthusiasm to brave the rigours of the North Sea no matter what season it is. However, on this, Tom's first visit, it was early March and both of us were yet to experience this delight.

Amidst the rubble strewn streets were a few shops catering for the army garrison and the married quarters of those El Ademites fortunate enough to have been allocated them. This was done by a sort of lottery, the rules of which were known only to the Air Ministry. These emporiums offered sheepskin rugs, Japanese cameras and flick knives (even flick combs too) all at very reasonable prices. Unlike popular myth, the shopkeepers did not wish to barter and must have grown bored having to repeat the article's original price ad nauseum until this was finally realised by each newcomer eager to acquire impossibly cheap items as portrayed in the movie *Casablanca*.

"Ah for Rick's friend we have special price."
Tom's face grew more perplexed as I in my self-appointed role of tour guide pointed out the few attractions or rather the many shortcomings the town had. I relished a certain amount of sadistic satisfaction as his bewilderment grew. Local inhabitants in their native costume of baggy trousers, old British army greatcoats and pulled down balaclavas went past giving further disenchantment to those who expected burnouse flowing sheiks with gold encrusted curved daggers. Suddenly Tom's sullen countenance became more animated and his eyes gleamed with the wicked look that had made many a girl capitulate to his charms.

Walking in front of us, dressed in what appeared from behind to be a black headscarf, a pretty pink blouse and a knee-length brown skirt, was a shapely looking female. Summoning his best mating cry Tom sprang into action. The startled girl turned around and he was met by a face completely hidden behind a sort of medieval executioner's mask. She was a well-known figure around the town, and although influenced by Western fashion bodily wise, she drew the line at exposing her face. Deterred for only a nanosecond by this forbidding cowl Tom pursued this promising looking Fry's Turkish Delight commercial. He knew a girl when he saw one. Everything was OK after all. An ugly silence reminiscent of the preliminary to a Western gunfight just before the clock strikes noon pervaded the atmosphere of the street.

As the girl ducked hurriedly down a narrow menacing alley Tom, oblivious to the changed ambience, and with the bit of ardour firmly between his teeth, started to follow her. I forcibly dragged him away fear lending unusual strength to my arms as he dwarfed me by several inches and a lot of pounds. I frantically explained in as forceful a manner as possible that if he continued pressing his amorous advances his, and more importantly my, life would not be worth a drilled piastre, (lowest denomination of the local currency). Still muttering disbelievingly, he allowed me to lead him to the town's only restaurant which was an Italian cafe specialising in what seemed to be camel bolognaise. Looking back on this I like to think I saved him from a nasty death, or at the least, emasculation.

    Drinking every night at the NA.FI could take its toll if one had to work the next day. Tom, being something of a mechanical genius, found the answer to this problem. His trade was that of teleprinter mechanic and he serviced the machines we operated. Unlike the rest of us in the hut he did not work shifts but had a more or less normal working day. If, however, a machine broke down during the night he would be called out away from his bed to repair or replace it. This meant that he would be allowed to make up his lost sleep the following day and come into work late.

Walking into the teleprinter room early one evening I came across him making minor adjustments to a clattering printer.

"Hello, Tom, I didn't know you had been called out!" I said surprised but pleased to have his company. Casting a furtive look at the door he replied, "Keep it cool man I ain't been called out."

He then explained that he would be attending a serious drinking session later that evening and would rather be dragged out to repair the machine about one a.m. when he was still awake and be allowed a nice lie in the following day. At zero forty-five precisely the afore mentioned machine became garbled and Tom was duly called out. An even more genial guy than usual danced into work (he never became an unsteady drunk), adjusted a little nut, and the indecipherable print smoothed into perfect legibility as though touched by Dr Who's sonic screwdriver.

One of the CO's most appreciated projects was the swimming pool. El Adem is situated about sixteen miles from the coast so a pool on the camp would have been a boon to morale. Before he ruled the camp, a pool had been under construction, but for some reason had been abandoned half completed. Thus, having the exact opposite effect as it was a constant reminder of what might have been. Having had first-hand experience of the ingenuity and expertise of the Airfield Construction Squadron the CO gave the task to them. True to form they came up with the goods. By the time the hot weather set in, about the end of March, we had our own swimming pool. You could not land an aeroplane on it, not even a sea plane, but we spent a lot of our off-duty hours there. How these building skills were part of the Airfield Constructions Squadron's duties I would hardly like to guess. I never saw them making any airfields or repairing our runway during the two years I was there but will always remember them and the CO with a sun-baked gratitude.

This oasis became the setting for many a bout of good-natured horseplay — people being thrown fully clothed into the chlorine scented depths was almost a daily occurrence. A few married women who braved the trip from Tobruk to bask in the waters had to suffer frustrated stares that glared with the intensity of the overhead sun. Of course, they were always accompanied by muscle-bound husbands whose vigilance matched that of King Idris's harem guards (Colonel Gaddafi's predecessor).

One day, as we all gazed at and fantasized about these unattainable forms, Tom casually stood up from lying beside the pool and said, "Just going to meet someone from Blighty, man. See you later."

We all exchanged bemused glances. What on earth was he babbling about? There were no new arrivals expected and all aircraft stopping here only paused long enough to refuel, raid our tax-free gift shop and hastily depart. Half an hour later Tom swanned back into the pool area and to our disbelieving eyes his arm was draped possessively around the shoulders of an attractive girl. There were never any serious outbreaks of racial tension at El Adem but due to our extreme envy it was stretched to breaking point at that moment. It was the case that Tom's friend was a WAAF who had been stationed with him in the UK and they had kept in touch. On being posted to Singapore she had written to him and arranged a meeting when the plane made its whistle stop at our forgotten outpost. After a few drinks they left for the departure lounge and what happened in the hour before take-off was the subject of much speculation. Whatever the outcome, to have arranged a date in our female starved community was some coup, but a typical example of Tom's popularity with the opposite sex and his resourcefulness.

Years later whilst working for British Telecomms as a customer service operator a woman called me who wanted a facility for cheap international phone calls to Antigua. In my efforts to personalise the call I asked her, knowing it was a small island, if she had ever met a guy called Leonard Thomas.

To my utter and amazed delight, she replied, "Good looking, clever and joined the RAF."

Chapter Eleven
Meanwhile Back in Blighty

A *Dear John* is an expression familiar to all when used to describe a brush off letter from a supposed loved one. At El Adem the expression took on new dimensions. Letters from home were awaited with the same breathless expectancy applied to my Social Security cheque. Sometimes the ancient DC6 that flapped its erratic way onto our camel-invaded runway to deliver the mail would be delayed by sandstorms that lasted days at a time. During those bleak times the queue at the NAAFI became even more congested than usual. Those who received such unwelcome communications, the format of which changed only in the degree of literacy, employed would react in various ways.

Some would become introverted and sullenly consume strong spirits whilst gazing into the amber depths with tortured eyes. Others would get fighting drunk and a few would do both. But by far the most popular was to pin the offending pages, which nearly always contained the sentence, *'You're too good for me'*, to the noticeboard of the mess where it received the written comments of the casual passer-by, a pen being suspended from the noticeboard for that purpose. These criticisms, mainly of an earthy nature, were nevertheless of greater originality and amusing turn of phrase than the displayed missive and must have been of great comfort to the *Dear Johns*.

Pat Boone's immortal ballad of the same name became the most requested spun disc on our internal broadcasting system. A week without his creamy smooth voice announcing, 'Dear John, oh how I hate to write!' being almost unknown. My mind baulks at what

Pete Flattery or Andy Legge would have done had it ever been requested for their ears.

Having literary pretensions even then, my advice was sometimes consulted when a romantic situation arose from perfume scented notepaper and a suitable turn of phrase was required. This was ludicrous really, my experiences so far being confined to back lane fumblings rather than sophisticated *affairs* Taxing my imagination to its limit I would dictate this pseudo amorous prose even plagiarising lines from popular songs. What the girl thought who read, 'I got stung, one night, loving you, don't be cruel to a fool such as I', gives me an embarrassed flush to this day as the whole sentence was made up of Elvis Presley song titles printed on the back of the album.

My own family and friends back home never ceased communicating in various ways. Freda Brown, my pet chameleon's namesake, wrote an entire letter on a pink toilet roll, the leaves of which were still stuck together and wound out like a colourful Christmas decoration. Her efforts may have been inspired by Steve McKay's effort. This arrived in the form of an imposing scroll complete with official looking seal. The contents were worded as a fictitious dispatch from the Emperor Nero to his then governor of Libya. We exchanged many messages in this style continually thinking up more novel ways to outdo each other with them.

Some of the more salacious letters from girlfriends would be passed around the entire camp and their graphic sexuality read in the latrines with the same concentration applied to the dirty postcards purchased from the market in Tobruk. I shudder to think what these early authors of soft porn would have thought had they realised the size of their circulation. Tape recordings were an innovation my family introduced. Making up in content and enthusiasm what they lacked in engineering these spoken messages would be played to an unexpectedly eager and definitely captive audience. Amusing anecdotes of daily life or community singing accompanied by my father's guitar would pervade the still desert air — someone once insisting that it was the original Burl Ives recording and not my father singing and playing *Little Bitty Tear*. The tapes returned by us were not as interesting as those received because those events we dared to relate occurred too infrequently and the remaining routine of our boring existence was not exactly riveting stuff. To compensate for this the aid of all and sundry was enlisted. Surprisingly there were never any refusals. Anyone asked would be only too willing to hold conversations with my family. I remember the second Christmas of my stay a poignant message of seasonal well-meaning from George Mason particularly impressing my mother with its obvious sincerity. With suppressed emotion inflecting his Cockney accent, George spoke quite ordinary and polite sentiments to her but the longing in his voice was all too apparent. Years later my mother was surprised and interested to learn that, authentic accent or not, George was black. His voice having given her a completely different mental image of his appearance as immigrants who had lived in Britain long enough to acquire a regional accent were a rarity in those days.

Chapter Twelve
Leave and Return

Some six months passed with unimaginable slowness before I accumulated enough leave to make a trip home of any enjoyable duration. The great day finally dawned. Armed with the contents of my bank book and four sets of Japanese silk pyjamas which were gifts for my female acquaintances, one of them being my mother, I ran up the gangplank of the Britannia aircraft misnamed *Whispering Giant* and with hungry eyes pressed to a port hole willed it to greater acceleration.

This holiday of six weeks flew past in a pleasant blur marred only by the time taken to adjust to the natives' complexions. Not a deliberate sneering comparison to my own suntanned skin, this was an almost subconscious awareness of what seemed to be an unhealthy grey pallor adorning the English faces I had spent so many months waiting to see. It was most apparent in the girls and the effect was heightened by make-up which gave the eerie illusion of hovering in front of their faces rather than actually touching the skin. In the words of George Harrison, 'All things must pass', and with empty heart, and even emptier wallet, I returned with reluctant feet back to the questionable charms of Libya stopping overnight en route at Malta.

On meeting a colleague whose self-pitying face mirrored my own, we pooled our resources, which meant I borrowed money from him, and we went out to sample the nightlife of nearby Valetta. The most heavily frequented area at that time was a series of narrow winding streets all of steep incline known graphically and affectionately by its multi-national visitors, which included sailors from all over the world and British military personnel, as, 'The Gut'. Here bars with gaudy lights and blaring jukeboxes ranked row upon row and competed with each other in unceasing efforts to relieve us suckers of our ackers, Selecting the nearest as being as good as any other we entered the garish portals.

From somewhere within the purple lit interior the booming, but by then outmoded, tones of Paul Anka implored us to put our heads on his shoulder, or some similarly impossible feat — he being an idol of enduring popularity in Malta and possibly still is. Meanwhile, be-sequinned hostesses of somewhat advanced years beckoned us to sit down. It was in this disreputable establishment that I first experienced the doubtful pleasure of a hot hand on my thigh and the whispered time-honoured inducement, "Buy me a drink dearie".

Being too frightened to do anything else and never having experienced such bold actions before from females, I did so. This was my first mistake. My second was to tip the waiter on his return when so entreated to by my gaudy companion because, on each of his many frequent trips thereafter with the cold tea masquerading as Scotch and imbibed by the girls with limitless capacity, he expected similar recompense. My third and final mistake was to try and keep up with the girl's speedy elbows whilst I drank a local aniseed flavoured strong drink called ouzo which has a kick like the Triumph Bonnevilles so favoured by the motorcycle fraternity of the Sixties. His feet an agile blur, the waiter replenished our drinks with a speed Usain Bolt would envy. As the night wore on, the wicked drink worked its evil spell.

A warm feeling of bonhomie pervaded the smoky air and both my comrade and me started making hopeful overtures to our female companions whose charms seemed to be magically increasing with every passing moment. Informing our naïve ears that the management of the club frowned on their employees just up and leaving the premises in mid-flow as it were, they said a toll was to be exacted. This was in the form of (and I cringe at the recollection) buying a bottle of cherry brandy for each hostess whose company the bar was being deprived of. Soliciting further funds from my companion I made the necessary purchase along with his. The two bottles were brought over and, to our surprise, we were expected to drink them there and then from the large beer schooners provided. Downing this brew is the last coherent memory of the evening. Waking up in the gutter several streets away some time later and during the small hours we both made an unsteady journey back to the transit accommodation for a few hours' sleep — our plane departing at nine a.m. that day.

Gritty eyed, we stumbled aboard the ancient DC6 — ruminating the while on the vagaries of cruel fate, we exchanged opinions on the previous night's eventful entertainment. The dubious attractions of our evening's partners had diminished considerably in the eye smarting brightness of day, and all things considered, we concluded that we had been let off pretty lightly.

Motors coughing spasmodically, our chariot jerked its aged frame to the end of the runway. My hungover head began to clear with fear induced rapidity as, looking out of the nearby window, I noticed the wings going up and down in a loose looking motion that matched the rhythm of the revving engines. After some minutes of this hardly confidence boosting activity, the brakes were released and with a Kamakzi howl the machine clawed its way off the heat blistered tarmac. Understandably I suffered a degree of depression on returning to the bedbug infested frame of my lonely cot. This was soon dispelled by a relatively minor incident that tickled my boyish sense of humour.

During the summer we all wore KD. This was a khaki-coloured tropical outfit of shirts and shorts, no doubt inspired by Baden Powell's apparel (founder of the Boy Scout movement) during the siege of Mafeking in 1899. The allowed official length of these voluminous shorts was supposed to be just above the knee. At that time nobody in their right mind would wish to present such a spectacle, and as one man we cut them down to an airy crutch exposing level, much to the embarrassment of our resident WVS woman as her mild eyes were sometimes subjected to the unexpected exposure of various sized pudenda whilst their owners sat down to peruse her kindly donated periodicals. Lacking the patience or the sewing skill to alter my own shorts, I merely tucked up the material to the desired length and then ran around this large hem with a stapler. On entering the mess one day I was singled out for attention by the station warrant officer, known with that acronym habit of the military as the SWO.

A SWO is the RAF equivalent of the army's regimental sergeant major and always enjoys a similar position of power and disposition to those discipline loving gentlemen. In the main the pettier forms of restriction relating to appearance and dress were relaxed by those in command. They probably realised these strictures were unnecessary and, in our case, rather inadequate anyway. Of course, this sort of control was the main reason for the SWO's existence and, to justify his position, a sporadic bout or two would be indulged in. And on this occasion I was elected. With his rigidly starched pair of baggy Badens straining to reach his ankles he pointed with outraged swagger stick at my own scantily clad thighs conveniently ignoring scores of similarly dressed men who were hastily scurrying past with averted eyes.

"Those shorts are of incorrect length, Airman. Stand to attention so I can see just how short they are." This I did, quelling a mad impulse to burst into hysterical laughter of the kind usually experienced in church during the sermon. On closer observation he noticed the worst.

"My god, not only are they too short you've held up the hem with staples. And (this last uttered with a whisper of total disbelief as the biggest sin of all as all bits of metal on military uniforms must shine as bright as a nova sun) they're rusty!"

The next day, I suffered the mild inconvenience of parading in his office dressed in the desired style with no sense of bitterness. Suffering a severe dressing down, I then duly stapled my shorts back up again on my return. But the morale boosting antics of the SWO proved to be just the tonic I needed and I was able to face the empty months ahead with some measure of fortitude. I will always be grateful to him.

Chapter Thirteen
Tropical Nights

Paddy, or Spud, Murphy was a son of Ireland with the voice of an angel and the temper of Robert De Niro's character in *Raging Bull*. In his day he had been a boxer of some repute and then, ten years later, still wrapped his torso in cellophane and ran around the camp to lose extra calories gained from whiskey with beer chasers which he was very partial to. Paddy organised a boxing tournament with Cyprus and, despite the fact that my physique resembled the 'before' of a Charles Atlas bodybuilding course, he asked me if I would like to go and be a competitor. The lure of the iniquitous pursuits available in Nicosia did loom up temptingly for a moment but rank cowardice triumphed. I declined his kindly offer and, like Marlon Brando's character in *On The Waterfront*, was reduced to, "I could have been a contender". We had been friends when stationed together in Middlesex so we naturally indulged in the odd booze up together and it was he who introduced me to the remnants of the *Afrika Korps*.

Some three miles from our remote township was another huddle of huts known to us as German Town. Its inhabitants were all of German nationality and of the generation who helped Rommel create such successful mayhem in Libya during World War II. Their method of making a living is still slightly obscure but I would hazard a guess that they were some kind of oil workers although at that time Libya's oil industry was not fully developed. Whether these bronzed blonde Teutons had returned to the scene of their former activity for political reasons or simply stayed on when the Eighty Army dispersed the rest of their comrades I am not certain. The sight of one of these men complete with forage cap driving a restored German wartime jeep, the bodywork ingeniously repaired with old ammunition boxes, was an interesting but slightly disquieting spectacle. You got the impression that parked out of sight behind the dunes an armoured column daubed in black crosses only awaited his return from a scouting 'recce' to roar into blazing vengeful action.

This of course was a completely unjustified fantasy. The hospitality of these men was legendary. Many a night of revelry was spent in their town's bar. This popularity was possibly helped by their store of imported and highly potent German beer which had the added attraction of being bottled. I recall with thirsty nostalgia the moisture beaded green glass of those ice-cold bottles.

After warming up by consuming the odd gallon of this brew and indulging in a few successful bouts of arm wrestling, Paddy would begin to sing. No typical Irish tenor he — his influences were Italian — and out of that pugilistic frame would pour well-known arias such as performed by Gilli, Caruso and other great tenors. Despite its incongruity the memory of an Irish Catholic with republican sympathies singing Verdi or Puccini to an audience of ex-German soldiers in the middle of the Libyan desert is a very wistful one.

Unfortunately, some overbearing boors, possibly from our catering section, visited German Town one night and tried to emulate Montgomery's successful campaign of El Alamein. They pathetically failed and were duly routed by these tough veterans. But our authorities heard about it and, like the bordellos of Singapore, German Town was declared a forbidden zone. This did not deter Paddy, though, who made numerous illicit treks across the pitch-black desert to a hearty welcome. The rest of us, having been allowed transport before, were a little less eager. This reluctance not being due to any misplaced respect for authority but mines and various other anti-personnel devices still abounded in the soil from the war.

We often heard them exploding spontaneously as the metal cooled after a hot day, and to suffer the possibility of an ironic emasculation was a much greater deterrent than any dictate of standing orders.

Another restricted area was the living quarters of the female NAAFI employees.

An incident that led to this point being heavily re-emphasised happened like this. Every community has its Don Juan and ours was no exception. Cast in the mould of the then current pop stars he was a particularly handsome example of his breed named after his style: *Flash.* Unable to further his notoriety in our straitened circumstances, Flash would regale his cronies with tales of more fruitful days, strumming moodily on his guitar and occasionally breaking into an Elvis Presley song of whom he could do a very passable imitation.

NAAFI workers, like all of us, served a sentence of two years and were then replaced by a new intake. Two new girls were duly flown in one day and with practiced ease Flash curled his lip in the manner of his idol, set his broad shoulders with his best James Dean slouch and swung into action.

Although being in the enviable position of being able to choose their paramours from hundreds of fawning suitors, the girls stood no chance against Flash's truculent charm. Within days of arriving, and despite stern warnings from the NAAFI manageress, (she too knew about Flash's reputation), they succumbed to his sneering grin of even white teeth. Tales of wild parties held by Flash and his crowd of privileged hangers-on began to circulate enviously around the camp. Held surreptitiously in the girls' rooms, which fortunately were out of earshot of the manageress' quarters, these debaucheries enjoyed a reign of some weeks. Possibly growing over confident due to their undetected activities, the festivities became wilder and the volume increased proportionately. Finally disturbed by the noise, the manageress staged a raid.

She flung open the door and a scene of wild abandon akin to those held by patrons of a Chicago speakeasy during the USA's Prohibition era greeted her outraged authoritarian stare. Members of both sexes, whose dress was in various stages of disarray, capered uninhibitedly to the strains of the Shadows pounding out the primitive rhythm of 'The Savage'. Immediately her dampening presence was realised, a confused hasty retreat was made by the male members of the Bacchanalian orgy. Jumping through windows, running down corridors and hastily scaling the eight-foot-high barbed wire fence that encircled the building, they fled back to the austerity and safety of their stale sock smelling bachelors' quarters. In all the scrambling confusion, Flash, in an unusual moment of modesty, must have thought he was inconspicuous and, still hopeful of continuing these amorous adventures later, when the heat died down, hid himself in a wardrobe. His optimism was short lived.

Having restored order to a level of at least surface respectability the manageress began a thorough search in the best tradition of Brian Rix bedroom farces. As she opened the door of his hiding place, knowing the jig was up, Flash treated her to his famous grin and, with a genial, "Good evening", stepped out of the wardrobe, walked with one graceful unhurried stride through a conveniently open window and sauntered off into the night, guitar in hand. Drastic action was taken. The hapless girls were deported in disgrace to home and dismissal. What the ecclesiastical parent of one of the girls made of all this is a matter I often ruminate on in moments of idle nostalgic speculation.

One woman who never suffered the attentions of over sexed suitors was the WVS woman. This matronly figure of some fifty-three summers, used to hold court in the WVS lounge attached to the AAFI. There was a distinct contrast from the bawdy singing crowd in the bar only some ten feet away and this quiet little kingdom over which she ruled with a maternal but firm hand. Her main method of looking after our welfare was supplying the room with magazines of a very innocuous nature and the out-of-date newspapers with which we kept up with events back home. No liquid stronger than coffee was allowed to be consumed in her little haven whose air of tranquillity was broken only by the quietly played records requested by the mild-mannered clients of her homely domain. I still possess an old Marty Wilde album she donated to my collection knowing it was a disc I repeatedly asked her to play, (my musical taste at that time perhaps understandably tending to the teenage angst variety). A completely harmless but noisy gathering did on one occasion shatter the sepulchral calm of this library-like room in the unlikely but welcome persons of Flash and Curly.

Curly was a temporarily posted in mechanic who was attached to a fighter squadron sent out to enjoy pseudo dog fights with one another in the cloud-free skies that shimmered above our sun pounded village. Being a talented guitarist and vocalist, he naturally attracted the attention of Flash, who, working on the premise, 'If you can't beat 'em join 'em', teamed up with Curly in many an impromptu concert at their respective huts. By now with the Beatles at its head, the so-called *Mersey Sound* was making serious inroads into the established rock scene of which Curly, having just come from the UK, was a highly skilled exponent. One day a notice was displayed in the WV lounge:

Jamming Tonite With Flash and Curly.

Starved of any form of live entertainment, the camp's resident and Shadows influenced group being mainly engaged at the officers' mess, the room became packed with crowds of men good naturedly suffering the privation of Pepsi Cola and tea in the cause of showbiz. Dressed in their usual informal garb of ripped T-shirts cut down denim jeans and straw cowboy hats, Flash and Curly sat in a corner, nodded to one another and 'took off'. Only then was the depth of Curly's talent revealed. Running the gamut of any current hit requested, Curly played with an authority awesome to behold. Having exhausted every known artistes' songs, from Bill Haley to Gerry and the Pacemakers, he launched into other areas. Fingers running effortlessly around the fretboard, he played Spanish flamenco and then to tumultuous applause changed to a medley of well-known jazz standards. Singing the vocals and shouting the unfamiliar chord changes to Flash his ability dwarfed any of the musicians who accompanied the CSE performers. After continuous request by the WVS woman to play a soft romantic song, he ended the performance by sitting on her desk and singing a soulful version of 'Lonesome Town' recorded by Ricky Nelson. Of all the more sober moments remembered from El Adem, the night Flash and Curly gigged at the WVS room is one of the most treasured. Another, but not so sober, is of when a party was held at the beach club in Tobruk. On this particular evening the camp's group performed there at (for want of a better word) a dance.

Those were the days when a group would know about twelve songs and, having exhausted this list, would start again. With no thought of setting what has become a current trend but necessitated by a lack of available female partners most of the men danced with each other. This sea of sweaty males with the odd woman tossed around like highly-prized driftwood was surging in full tide to the third encore of 'Apache' when interrupted by the inimitable Curly.

Like a character in one of those early rock 'n' roll movies, his friends were urging him to stand up with the band and add a few numbers to the group's modest and oft repeated repertoire. In Curly's case, stopping him would have been harder. Giving the understandably reluctant guitarist a wad of Libyan currency as a deposit against any damage to the instrument, he leapt up on the stage, muttered a key to the band and kicked off with the Beatles' 'Please Please Me'. Up to now his audience had only heard him play acoustically, now amplified he had even more impact.

Responding with the raw fervour of the Sioux nation on the eve of Custer's Last Stand the dancers shook and twisted with inexhaustive energy. After a half hour of this pounding upstaging, the group began to flag as keeping up with Curly was stretching their abilities to the limits, so he concluded by playing an instrumental version of 'Hava Nagila' — climaxing by playing the chorus with the guitar held behind his head whilst he ran on the spot in time to the beat. Carried from the stage on a wall of applause and the shoulders of the crown, Curly was feted in the manner of a homecoming Olympic medal winner.

Chapter Fourteen
Salad Days

When the relative safety of the swimming pool became a little mundane, the aquatically inclined would spend a day in the sea at Tobruk. Knowing that scantily clad wives would outrage the local inhabitants' sense of morality, a beach was allocated presumably by the Libyan authorities exclusively for our own use. It's hard to believe in retrospect that people pay thousands of hard-earned pounds to indulge in a pastime we took for granted. Of course, like Daniel Defoe's famous character, we would have all paid to leave.

Our Mediterranean playground did not exactly rival the Côte d'Azur which paralleled it across the waters to southern France in either service, or hordes of basking bathing beauties but it did have a beach club with a bar. Any relaxing activity not including alcohol was severely frowned on by all.

They even served beer in the airmen's mess, an unheard-of precedent anywhere else which was probably initiated by our beloved CO.

Swimming around wearing fins and snorkels whilst gazing at the fascinating and colourful world below nearly usurped masturbation as my favourite pastime. No television documentary can truly reproduce the reality of observing underwater sea life first hand. The depth of colour alone is something that will be rhapsodised on by more talented writers than I. Suffice to say it was truly beautiful.

Because I was a shift worker, I would often indulge in this activity straight from night duty as the sea was so tranquil and silent, making it more comfortable than my itching mosquito net draped bed. This rather dangerous habit did have its disadvantages. Whilst cruising around gazing at the smoothly moving fish and gently waving underwater plants below I would doze off whilst lying on my face and breathing through a snorkel. I would wake up completely disorientated and thrashing about like a freshly netted cod. On occasion this could prove to be inconvenient, as I usually got carried out quite far by the current in unsuspecting oblivion and would have a long swim back to land.

In my oceanic perambulations I would come across sticks of bombs lying embedded nose first in the seabed. These were further mementos of the war left with gay abandon by the older generation who, for all their lecturing moralising about sex, seemed to have had a lackadaisical attitude towards their hardware bordering on the irresponsible. One day, I was following a shoal of fish who became aware of me and started to swim faster away from me thinking I was some large predator. Suddenly, they all turned and came rushing back. I got curious and looked beyond them realising that they considered something more dangerous than I was a threat to them and were fleeing accordingly. I was right.

Swimming towards me was what appeared to be a four-foot-wide mouth. They say watching tropical fish around a well-lit tank is one of the most relaxing of pastimes. When you are one of the fish and you think a larger one has you earmarked for lunch, the exact opposite applies. Emulating the behaviour of my fellow refugees I turned around and, with my fastest crawl, broke all known freestyle Olympic records to the safety of the nearby shore. As I was sitting on the ground congratulating myself on escaping the fate of Captain Ahab, I noticed some aqualung enthusiasts nearby who were preparing to board a motor launch and go exploring. I went across to them and, after I described *The Beast From Twenty Thousand Fathoms* they all roared with laughter. It appeared that this *Moby Dick* who had inspired my fear-crazed flight was nothing more than a harmless grouper. As the grouper is virtually toothless, the worst it could do was give me a nasty suck.

One night, I had just completed an evening shift and had returned from work to continue my ceaseless war with Africa's insect life. Outside the hut I came across Ted Evans who was sitting in a car and was accompanied by several of his drinking companions. A skilled motor mechanic, his services were often called upon by the officers to repair their private cars for which they would pay a reasonable fee. Had they realised the type of road test he subjected their vehicles to they might have been more cautious in giving him custody of their prized possessions.

It was now a quarter to midnight but Ted and his fellows, in their search for more novel ways of consuming their daily intake of life preserving nectar, were bent on a moonlight swimming and drinking party. As transport they were going to use the Austin Mini Ted was currently fixing. Having the next morning off, it only took a short persuasion for me to accept their invitation to join them. With six of us piled into a vehicle that was meant for four, the conditions were a little cramped but as they were all very far from sober nobody cared. We roared off down the long road to Tobruk and, noticing the speedy but erratic course Ted set, I hastily drank several cans so like the rest I would consider this danger beneath notice.

On leaving the desert plateau and making our way down the dangerous road to the coast, Ted took great delight in accelerating towards an approaching bend then slamming on the brakes at the last possible moment. This would make the car skid around the corner in approved Grand Prix fashion.

The majority greeted these actions with shouts of approval but the sight of the little white stones, the only barrier between us and a drop of hundreds of feet, hurtling past made me sincerely regret my impulsive trip as I was not yet quite as inebriated as my carefree companions. God is supposed to smile on children and drunks I am told. Well, he must have been beaming from ear to ear that night because we made it to the sea.

There was no mishap to mar the occasion apart from one small incident. In between swims and drinks, we lost one of us. This was a Scotsman called McGee. A native of Glasgow, he was noted for an ability to cause havoc and mayhem whenever he went drinking but always emerging completely unscathed from these adventures. After some time frolicking in the warm surf, we decided to go back to camp and then noticed he had disappeared. We did a token five-minute search but soon tired of this and, with the careless optimism of all drunks, made our way home thinking he would be all right,

We never learned the full story because all McGee remembered was waking up in the local gaol. This was a somewhat primitive affair. The plank he woke up on fulfilling the function of a bed. His previous hilarity somewhat dissipated by now, McGee screamed loudly about what he considered a high-handed action by the

Libyan police. His cries were noted by the khaki clad constabulary — this being the local drunk tank they told him to just lie down and sleep it off. With one look at the uninviting plank lying on top of the mud floor he had just vacated, McGee declined and insisted they release him.

With his usual luck, or maybe it was anything for a quiet life, this is exactly what they did. He sat beside the road for two hours and caught the early bus from Tobruk that ferried the married men who lived there to work at El Adem.

Chapter Fifteen
Lulls in the Storm

In a desperate attempt to dispel the grinding boredom I volunteered my services as part-time waiter in the officers' mess. These duties being extra to normal I received three shillings an hour for them. This may seem, even allowing for inflation, as rather a small sum but as the privileged sect held dining in nights that went on into the small hours, this self-imposed occupational therapy proved quite lucrative.

There were other perks. The cuisine of this establishment when compared to ours made a contrast akin to that offered by the London Savoy Grill against that of the maggot infested delicacies esteemed by some Eskimo tribes. Years later, whilst stationed in Singapore with every known entertainment and vice practised by humanity easily available, I would be bewildered by the vagaries of the military mind as I queued in the mural decorated dining hall where thirty choices of meal cooked to a very high standard was available every lunch hour.

Turned out in a white shirt and black bow tie with a drooping RAF cummerbund draped around my waist,

I would flit around the mess with an ever-alert eye to the main chance. No six-course dinner was served without my consuming at least eight along with the appropriate wines. Prior to this I had never known anything more exotic than brandy with ginger ale. Dry martinis, Bordeaux, Reisling and single malt Scotch were all poured down my eager throat with complete disregard to the convention of not mixing liquors. Some nights after dinner was over I would be asked to serve behind the bar giving my alcoholic delinquency free reign, even supplementing it legitimately as drinks were bought for me by the more generous natured of the clientele. Growing bolder with each success, my insolence knew no limits until the evening which celebrated the arrival of the new CO.

The meal served that night was of particular excellence. I had starved myself all day in greedy anticipation which was no real hardship considering the unappetizing fare I had forsaken. It was with even more voracious gusto than usual that I surreptitiously attacked the toothsome delicacies bedecking the groaning buffet tables. When all were replete the officers and their ladies retired to the lounge which doubled as a ballroom and danced to the amplified instrumentations of the camp's pop group. My job being that of floor waiter giving me ample opportunity to watch first-hand the abortive attempts made to dance the twist then in vogue. The combination of too much food and drink plus their (in my opinion) stealing of a slice of youth culture whilst I, a fully-fledged member of that society, had to look on from the sidelines, led to a growing feeling of resentment at these ungainly gyrations.

This was given a chance to burst out in open rebellion. Unable to stand the pace of the unaccustomed exercise, one middle-aged gentleman, the civilian meteorological officer I believe, abandoned his wife on the dance floor and retired to his seat with a relieved sweaty sigh. The woman herself seemed reluctant to leave the floor. With an unthinking rhythmic bound I came to her rescue. Feet twisting to the beat and arms and torso moving in the correct towelling dry action I demonstrated the exact spine rupturing technique employed by my US contemporaries. Sadly, or rather poetically, justifiably this triumph was short lived.

On leaving work that night I was not disciplined in any way (my employers were always politely distant with their domestic help) but was told that the staff shortages that had given me the chance of work were now over and my services would no longer be required. I philosophically accepted my last wage packet and made my way to a nearby hut where another form of escapism was practiced. Gambling.

Not being subject to any large customs and excise duty booze, cigarettes and other such necessities were all available at ridiculously low prices. Consequently, money was of minor importance to us all. This uncaring attitude to the filthy lucre led to large sums being frittered away on the turn on of a card with casual aplomb.

The game I joined had been in progress for some ten hours already but gambling infects its enthusiasts with its own peculiar brand of endurance, only leaving its practitioners leaden face and drained after the game finishes. Days can rush by before this happens, so it was an alert eyed school of some fifteen people who dealt and bet in a game of three-card brag.

Even for that hard-nosed school the play was deep. This was before the term 'inflation' became so well worn, yet the blind stake was ten shillings. To look at one's own hand the sum of one pound had to be deposited in the kitty illustrating the steep play as a pound was ten per cent of a week's wages. By simple reckoning two rounds of this and there could easily be an accumulated pot of over thirty pounds and there were numerous hands dealt.

Losing my night's wages in about ten minutes flat I stayed to watch the remaining players continue betting these vast sums across the blanket-covered table as the aforementioned fever infects spectators too. When the last bet was placed and the final kitty raked into its winner's beret the reckoning was totalled up for those who had used tokens rather than money. The largest loser was a small statured lad called Sean O'Toole. Like the Regency members of White's club or waiters he had been allowed unlimited credit, a man's honour in these matters being sacrosanct. With similar formality and cool demeanour to those rakes of old and with that gifted articulate dignity possessed by many Irishmen, he put a proposition to his creditors to whom he owed the collective sum of a hundred and eighty pounds.

"Gentlemen. I have here my savings book which as you can see contains four hundred pounds. I will cut the pack double or quits with each of you who hold my IOUs."

As one man they all agreed and with the nonchalance of James Garner in the role of *Maverick* he faced his poker faced adversaries. The pack was split six time and the only one he lost to was owed a mere ten pounds.

Chapter Sixteen
The Hitch-Hiker

European civilian visitors were an extremely rare species to grace our unwilling exile. I can only recall two such courageous travellers. One was an adventurous young woman who was possibly a member of the Will family, the well-known purveyors of Woodbine cigarettes and other forms of self-immolation. This advance guard of the women's liberation movement was engaged in a solo flight from Britain to Australia. Her stay lasted only long enough to allow for the refuelling of her small aircraft before zooming off into the blue horizon and the newspaper headlines. The other was on foot and, therefore, even more daring. This fair-haired giant had set off on a hitch-hiking journey from Sussex and he too was bound for Aussie land although at a more leisurely pace than the feminine Biggles who preceded him.

Even our jaundiced society was impressed by this boy's daring and pioneering attitude as this was years ahead of the hippie trail to the Far East. He was speedily smuggled into our camp and housed in one of our tin huts, the occupier whose bed he used being conveniently away raising Cain in the UK on leave. After a few days spent recuperating in these surroundings and being fed at the same time as our other pets he expressed a certain restlessness of spirit which we were all too familiar with.

Hoping to extend his freedom and simultaneously put one over on our superiors, a sport engaged in with never ceasing enthusiasm, we escorted him to our mess hall for lunch. The catering sergeant was a little more vigilant than to allow the presence of a six-foot blond-haired Beatle-topped stranger to go past unnoticed. Our newly adopted friend was taken away for a mild interrogation at the guard house. Once his identity and the purpose of his visit was established he was released, given a meal and allowed to continue his globe-trotting jaunt.

During our final conversation, I queried as to what employment he had been engaged in prior to commencing his international stroll. Anticipating something like mountaineering guide, football coach or deep-sea diver his wry reply was the least expected.

"I used to be a ladies' hairdresser but after years of their company you start to talk and act like the buggers. That's probably the reason why I nicked off. See you, Sport."

Chapter Seventeen
The Riot and Other Tensions

I have stated that there were no serious outbreaks of racial prejudice at El Adem but there was one example worthy of note because of its unlikelihood. A contingent of Maltese troops paid us a visit as they were participating in some manoeuvres involving the army. These swarthy Latins became a familiar sight in the NAAFI canteen each evening and were more or less accepted by all. By now our West Indian population had increased and naturally there was a tendency for this minority group to stick together. Our particular blacks all seemed to be jazz lovers, often congregating in each other's huts to play records, nodding their sunglass decorated foreheads to the musical virtuosity of Cannonbal Adderley, Miles Davis and Thelonius Monk. Having some similarity in skin tone it must have been some subtle cultural difference that led to our episode of racial violence because it occurred between these two factions. Whatever the cause, the Maltese and the blacks had it in for each other. Disdainful brown sneers were returned by even darker scowls and the tension mounted.

The night it snapped I was giving ear once more whilst in the WVCS lounge to the beloved voice of Marty Wilde as he bemoaned the fate of being a teenager in love. (Years later, to name drop, I met this early British rocker and got drunk with him and his band in a night club in my home town.) Thus as the lounge overlooked the patio of the NAAFI, I was granted a ringside seat at the ensuing skirmish. The particular incident that sparked off this clash escapes me but one minute everything seemed normal but the next all hell broke loose.

West Indians and Maltese were punching and kicking each other like extras in a John Wayne film. The action surged over and around the patio, a mixture of fighting, pummelling figures all crowded into the dimly lit square of the patio. How they could tell who was who, I have no idea. Little scenarios spring to memory. A West Indian hitting a Maltese with a table that shattered into pieces on impact. A very small Maltese boy running up behind a huge Jamaican and bouncing a long fire extinguisher off his adversary's head. The unfortunate recipient stiffening like a rigid pole and falling down unconscious in a manner I had up to then thought just part of Hollywood's more fanciful melodramatic presentations.

The sound of the arrival of our reluctant police force did break up this sporting affray just as bets were being placed on the outcome. The more seriously injured were taken to sick quarters to be patched up.

(One carried there in a wheelbarrow.) I have no memory of anyone actually being arrested. This may have been in an effort to avoid further outbreaks inflamed by unwelcome inquisitions. With that peculiar attitude practiced by men of violence, the two warring units became bosom friends after that. For the duration of the Maltese's stay they were frequently seen together in the bar joining in singsongs that featured tunes of Malta and the Caribbean.

A desert camp is a strange place to acquire an insight into the emotive politics of Northern Ireland but, as our society included a large contingent from the Emerald Isle, my education regarding this tortuous subject was considerably broadened. Although in those far-off days the then current IRA was a standing joke amongst both factions and it was long before the deadly confrontations of 1968 onwards. I became a bemused spectator to heated talks about 'B' Specials, Fenians and Orangemen. Being mainly Roman Catholic, the reasons a lot of these boys had joined up seemed to be the lack of work available to members of their faith. An exception to this was Corporal McGregor. His limbs tattooed with Union Jacks and patriotic slogans, this dark wiry Glaswegian was an Orangeman. Up until then I had connected this term with a mysterious fruiterers' convention held annually in Glasgow and Liverpool. Cpl McGregor's behaviour soon enlightened me. This dedicated patriot held distinctly strong loyalist views and an unrelenting intolerance towards Fenians or Republican supporters that, because of its exaggerated proportions, was more amusing than shocking.

His rank entitling him to his own private room, he would hold wild drunken solo political gatherings in his flag decorated room. Loud martial music would pour out of this lodge in Libyan exile whilst he ranted and raved to the empty walls like a dictator looking for a crowd. A stranger passing his room with the record player blasting and McGregor screaming slogans could easily have thought an enthusiastic rally of thousands was being held.

One of the melodies that continually disturbed the still air was the Glasgow Rangers' football song. Having no sympathy either way, but becoming mildly disturbed by these noisy conventions, I consulted Spud Murphy and asked him to teach me the Glasgow Celtic song. Whenever these loyalist orgies reach an unbearable level, I would sing the Celtic song through his keyhole and hurriedly scamper into the nearby washrooms. He would frantically unlock his door and with his beer mug decorated by the Queen's portrait clutched in one hand he would leap around the barrack block screaming, "Come out you bastard Fenian. Come out. I'll give ye death before dishonour."

After a decent interval I would walk boldly out of the washroom as he never associated my towel swathed figure with the hated rebel. Followed by his frustrated voice now subsiding into incoherent muttering I would return to my Tyneham with suppressed amusement.

This rather odd behaviour of Cpl MacGregor was probably his own form of safety valve. If so it was just as well because his trade was air traffic controller and the fate of hundreds was held in his flag-waving hands every day as he radioed final landing instructions to huge transport jets.

Chapter Eighteen
Brief Encounters

On the plateau above Tobruk lies a cemetery, a memorial to the dead of World War II. This sad reminder of a less peaceful era was passed every day by the traffic journeying to and from the camp. Idly gazing out of the bus window at the neat uniform rows on one of my numerous trips to the beach, I would ruminate on the even greater hardships endured by all those dead young men. Interspaced between the graves, field guns and anti-aircraft pieces pointed skyward as if in hope that an uninformed Stuka pilot would make a rather overdue appearance. My interest in this place went no further, but there were those who did visit it and walk amongst those too numerous headstones. One such visitor was one of my roommates Dave Stoneman.

Dave was from London, a tall thin be-freckled figure; we did not usually seek out each other's company, but thrown together by the journey we chatted amiably enough as the bus rattled along the uneven road. Nearing journey's end, Dave asked the driver to stop beside the cemetery gates. With Yashika and light meter slung around his neck and wearing his foreign correspondent's outfit of fawn slacks, bush shirt and floppy camouflaged hat, he swung off the bus to photograph the cemetery. I continued on to my ceaseless but futile pursuit of the Med's underwater inhabitants.

This was the day that brought to an end my dangerous habit of swimming in the sea straight after night shift. When I fancied a change of scene from the beach I would go diving in the harbour area. With the sea littered with the huge concrete remains of shattered World War II pillboxes it made a fascinating playground. The gun slits and apertures now being used as submarine passageways and doorways for the never-ending cavalcade of colourful fish. A function I considered far more constructive than their original use. But this day fate had some spice to add to things.

Just as I made a rather clumsy duck dive, one of my snorkels became detached from my face mask and the sea poured in. Simultaneously my right leg, overly tired from lack of sleep, decided to do just that. Severe cramp seized my calf muscles and one rubber flipper fell off.

To be brief, I was in danger of drowning. Still wracked by pain and hampered by the use of one leg, I somehow managed to reach the surface, rid myself of the remaining but encumbering flipper and swim toward the harbour wall with a sort of crippled butterfly stroke. A Libyan and his young son were standing on the quayside and, perceiving my difficulties, had come forward to help. I was then able to hand them the vision obscuring, water filled face mask and my spear gun which I had kept hold of in fear that if I dropped it, it might go off and add further complications by impaling me. This left both hands free to massage some life back in my leg whilst I trod water with the sound one. Circulation restored, I hauled myself on the quayside not exactly shaken to the core, but I felt it was a close thing.

Recovering myself and my flippers I tried to express my thanks for their timely assistance. My limited Arabic only running to obscenities and their English being only slightly better, this was mainly conducted in sign language but the gist was understood by all. I spent all day with them drinking the glasses of tea the father brewed on a casually lit fire.

After the day came to a close, I went for a meal in the Italian cafe coincidentally bumping into Dave Stoneman again.

The time of year was an important Moslem religious festival called the Feast of Ramadan. From sunrise to sunset the true believer is not allowed to eat or drink. Sunset was heralded by a cannon shot fired at about six p.m. As many of the cafe's customers were Libyans, we were treated to the sight of them all with eating utensil in hand hovering over their heaped plates waiting for this explosive permission to eat. This 'under starter's orders' sort of situation made us a bit self-conscious so we waited too.

The gun boomed and we worked our way through spaghetti bolognaise washed down with Belgian beer served in tall ice-cold green bottles. A nearby Libyan, having finally satisfied his day-long fast, nodded at us in a friendly fashion. We struck up a conversation with him and he joined us as we continued drinking bottle after bottle of this tasty brew which was the cafe's most attractive but exclusive feature. Several hours passed this way until our new friend suggested we adjourn to the town's only hotel where we could continue drinking long after the cafe had closed. This was promptly agreed upon and we ended up at this establishment drinking into the small hours.

Knowing the Moslem habit of making up for their refreshment-starved day by eating and drinking all night we were not unduly alarmed when he suggested we hire a room for the night and continue our revels via room service. We all staggered upstairs to this room, Dave and I not even becoming suspicious as to the rather inadequate sleeping facilities of only two beds. Further drinks were ordered and we drank on, blithely unaware of the inevitable.

When it came, I had reached the drowsy state of, if I closed my eyes too quickly, the room whirled a bit. Maybe this was the reason that Dave was the one whom our companion chose to try it on with or maybe I just had no appeal. Dave's rampant sexuality was illustrated by his girlfriend's letters which were a constant inspiration to all, so the amorous gentleman could not have made a more unfortunate choice.

I was rudely awakened from a light doze by Dave's outraged bellow.

"'Ere git orf you dirty bastard!"

Possibly thinking these were just the half-hearted coy gestures preceding a more willing acceptance, this representative of the Libyan Gay Front continued pressing his suit.

"Whatsa matta, John? We friends. C'mon."

With the pompous dignity of a Victorian school teacher castigating an infant for playing with himself Dave spelt it out.

"'Omosexuality mate, that's what!"

Rolling the syllables with great relish and shaking his fist under his would-be seducer's nose all the while. Recognising defeat, he departed, his efforts frustrated. But he had the last laugh.

We had to foot the bill for this further lesson in the ways of the wicked world.

Dave's own sexual leanings that amused our jaded tastes was his practice habit after working a night shift. Entering the warm fug-laden atmosphere of our little tin hut and thinking the other occupants were still asleep, he would quickly disrobe. Then, standing on his bed fully naked, he would fondle his thighs and nether regions making small animal noises of unbridled lust and clutching one of his girlfriend's salacious letters he would jump into bed making the walls vibrate in frenzied self-abuse. He was always observed by Pete Flattery who feigned sleep.

Some days, an inspection of our quarters would be carried out by an officer, thus necessitating the vacation of the room except for those sleeping off night shift. On those occasions we would all be awake on Dave's return, so his frustration would have to await our departure before being given release. Such was Pete Flattery's amusement that he would sneak back and look in the window catching up with us with mirth aglow face.

"Yes. He's started."

There was an element of hypocrisy in all this. The weariness of night shift made everyone randy and, coupled with our enforced celibacy, was even more intense. Someone once told me that the medical reason for this was the body releasing an extra flow of hormones to compensate for the exhaustion brought on by these night-long vigils. But, like the bromide sexual depressant supposedly and with futile effect stirred into our tea urns, this was probably just another myth.

Chapter Nineteen
Mystical Dabblings

Ron Goodwin was ahead of his time. A radio mechanic from Manchester he followed a personal philosophy of similar persuasion to that practised by the mid-sixties' flower children only his ideals were tempered by a rich Lancashire practicality. This strange mixture of black pudding wielding idealism attracted quite a following amongst us all. Anyone who can sink a crate of Watney's brown and expound, without slurring, about Dylan Thomas does have a certain fascination.

The booze and conversation were flowing easily one night when the subject of hypnosis arose. Stating that he had this power, Ron offered to send me into a trance and would use this ability to give me a pleasant experience revisited whilst I was asleep.

Any escape from El Adem even if only a spiritual one was welcome, so I volunteered.

Instructing me to lie down and requesting dim lights and silence he began his attempt to put me under. After ten minutes of being told how heavy my eyelids were and how sleepy I felt, I still remained as alert as six cans of Carlsberg lager would allow. Ron changed his tactics.

"Repeat after me the following," his level voice intoned.

"I feel very sleepy and so tired."

I started rather self-consciously to do so. By now a certain amount of restlessness could be sensed amongst the spectators. An easing of cramped limbs and various other small shuffling began to break the air of expectancy. Ignoring these fidgeting expressions of doubt, Ron droned on and I repeated the phrases. Suddenly it seemed an acoustic fault of the room was highlighted because, my parrot-like replies were being echoed. Ron's favourite drinking partner, an administration clerk called Robert Cummings, whilst sitting amongst the crowd had truly gone into a trance!

Silencing me with a hastily whispered, "Shurrup", Ron transferred his attentions to Bob.

Some months previously Bob, being in a position of power to do so, had engineered a trip to the Far East and spent a glorious time wallowing in Hong Kong's red-light district. Knowing this, Ron managed to help him relive the juicier moments to the envy of all present. On being awakened, Bob would not believe he had been in a trance insisting that he had just dropped off with boredom and had a pleasant dream about the Wanchai girls. Still arguing, he picked up his beret and placed it on his head upside down. As he started at his own peculiar action, we told him he had just carried out the post-hypnotic suggestion which Ron had implanted.

Some of Ron's abilities had a more practical application. Switching on my record player one day to play one of my four albums I was treated to the ear rending din of Elvis growling "You ain't nuthin' but a hound dawg",' backwards. My collection as in its infancy was somewhat limited, and tiring of incessant repetition, some wag had reversed the polarity of the motor. Not appreciating this attempt for variety, I asked Ron to reverse the reversal.

Commenting on the originality of the prankster with more professional appreciation than sympathy for my poor machine, this he did. But thereafter it somehow seemed to lack the desired metallic volume of before. The only reference to this anyone made was in the form of an anonymous request on the internal broadcasting system for Spike Milligan in the Goon character of Neddy Seagoon singing 'I'm Walking Backwards for Christmas'.

Drinking water was installed in long round concrete containers dotted around the camp, the contents renewed regularly by a truck that replenished them from a plant that processed the saline water. Always tepid, we used it mainly to make coffee brewed in our rooms with electric kettles or, for the more dangerously inventive, two church keys wired to an electric plug and dangled in the cup to be brewed. Some people made little businesses of this practice and one such unofficial cafe was run by Gordon Hyland. He lived in the barrack adjacent to mine and I became a regular customer.

Sitting in his bed space chatting with the other customers whilst listening to his Grundig tape-recorder play extremely well edited tapes of old seventy-eight records became a daily habit.

It was there that I first heard Chuck Berry belt out 'Sweet Little Sixteen' a sound that has had a profound effect on my life. After hearing this song I bought his album and on the album was 'Johnny B Goode'. Like a million other people, once I heard that song I went out and bought a guitar. As an alternative listening choice Gordon would sometimes play an erotic recording called 'The Honeymoon Express'. Loud train noises and whistles would be followed by a cry of, "All aboard".

The train would then chug out of the station and then simulated sounds of a couple engaged in rampant sexual intercourse would begin. We all laughed but there was a lot of wishful thinking tinging our mirth.

Another dweller in the barrack room greasy spoon was Bill Dowling, a friendly pipe smoking Yorkshireman. He surprised us all one day revealing an unexpected side to his character by doing exact impersonations of famous people and then of everyone present. What this mild-mannered thoughtful man had in common with a beat crazed teenager like myself leaves me baffled but we became firm friends. After he was allocated married quarters, he invited me to stay there overnight. I would take advantage of this open invitation whenever I felt particularly homesick. His wife, Babs, was just as friendly and made myself and Bob's other friend, Reg Turner, very welcome to spend an evening in the more comfortable surroundings of their flat in Tobruk.

Reg Turner was an exuberant type who loved fishing and was instructing Bill in the art of watching a bobbing float for hours in the hope that some unsuspecting fish would bite.

These fishing trips took place in the late evening. All four of us would walk down to the harbour, Bill and

Reg casting their rods, Babs to watch and, as the water was still warm, I to swim. At least one of the anglers would be successful and we would all troop back home with that pleasantly tired feeling such activities engender. We would stop on the way to buy freshly baked bread from the local bakery and Babs would cook the fish on our return.

Moments like those of a black velvet sky, decorated by brilliant stars whose light matched the phosphorescence of the warm sea gave a great feeling of contentment. I would always return from these trips refreshed and able to take the isolated rigours of camp with a reasonable amount of acceptance until the next bout laid me low.

Whilst making one of these morale boosting excursions, the journey of some forty minutes was unexpectedly lengthened. As previously described, the road to Tobruk is a single straight line across the desert with very little traffic. Not exactly a rival to the M1 (the UK's first motorway). Yet despite a view of approaching vehicles that stretched for miles, a pedestrian just like the man in the safety film stepped out in front of the bus. Somersaulting over several seats I fell in the aisle of the bus, luckily landing on my hands in a crouched position.

Wondering if the driver had a warped sense of humour, my immediate impulse was to hurl insults at his ancestry but, realizing something serious had happened, I stopped. The theory was that having an infallible faith in kismet or the will of God, the old Libyan gentleman would have stepped in front of a charging animal just as nonchalantly. Whether his belief in the preordained order was misplaced or not may be just an academic question as, whatever the truth, his action proved fatal.

Help was summoned from Tobruk along with a replacement bus. We all disembarked, skirting the sad bundle of old clothes lying on the hot tarmac. Maybe the old man's faith was correct as something good always seems to come from something bad and this was no exception. Although found completely blameless after the inquest was held, I heard that the driver was hurriedly repatriated in case the local citizens disagreed with the verdict.

Chapter Twenty
The Bomb Dump

Bomb dump guard was the least popular of our more military activities. The dump itself was located about two miles from the main camp and was reached by a rutted track masquerading as a road. The Land Rovers that brought the unwilling replacements tore along the uneven surface at a speed usually employed by the contestants in the Indianapolis Grand Prix. Necessitating an iron grip of the metal benches serving as seats as otherwise a hastier disembarkation than usually expected could befall you. Bouncing along this road to spend twenty-four sweating hours in a little round hut was one of our more futile duties. Although some courageous but mercenary minded people would willingly impersonate and take someone's place for the fee of a day's pay. Sadly, I was never solvent enough to make use of this highly illegal service except once as an employee.

On arrival at this wire-enclosed compound the relieved guard would clamber gratefully but wearily aboard. We would then divide the forthcoming time by tossing a coin to determine who did the night shift and then commence our defence of the rows of rusting bombs and stacked ammunition boxes. Despite the immediate proximity of all this explosive we were, in the paradoxical fashion of our commanders, completely unarmed. There were vague instructions as to which procedure to employ if any intruder appeared bent on ladening a donkey with a five-hundred pounder. In such an unlikely event, I hardly think, "Halt who goes there. Stop intruder or I will dial the guardroom", (two miles away remember) would have proved to be a successful deterrent.

The monotony of the duty was always broken by the flies, who in their search for sustenance, would even crawl up a recumbent sleeper's nostril. A particularly unpleasant way of being of wakened. An exception to this boring occupation was in the form of a telephoned order from the air traffic control Tower.

A V bomber was unable to make its final landing approach because a small herd of camels was blocking the runway. As I had drawn the daylight guard shift, I was ordered to clear them. Seizing a nearby fence pole I dutifully trotted off and chased these laconic looking creatures out of the path of Britain's main air defence arm. Not really minding the sweat-inducing exertion, because the idea of the fate of the jet age monster depending on me shouting, "Shoo go away" to three of four sarcastic looking camels rather tickled my fancy.

Just to keep up a semblance of a military organisation, these guard duties were preceded by a half-hearted parade held beside the guardroom situated at the main entrance to the camp. We had to don unfamiliar infantry equipment in the form of a webbing belt meant to be an attachment point for ammunition pouches which we never wore and, in fact, had never been shown how to assemble. Whilst waiting for the duty officer delegated to give us all a hurried glance for this farce, before he quickly drove off back to his mess, this unwilling squad would occupy the time by watching the Libyan labourers' departure. This was always good for a laugh because sometimes they were searched by the police in a vain-attempt to catch the spoils of the day's illicit takings. These workers would arrive in droves each morning, disappear into the depths of the camp, and reappear in the evening. What they did in the interim period is anyone's guess. Our own talent for skiving (avoiding work) was a highly developed art form but they outclassed us completely and their professional ease of toil avoidance was a much-admired skill. Mountains of empty wooden packing cases were utilised by these brilliant shirkers and converted into warren-like dens into which they disappeared only emerging to make the noon day devotions towards Mecca.

The frustrated antics of the works department as they made futile efforts to get some task carried out was a constant form of amusement. Their pilfering prowess was legendary so our police, who made Sherlock Holmes' long suffering Scotland Yard Inspector Lestrade look like a crime detecting genius, had no chance. The workers stood in a line as they were searched and the ones at the end of the line passed any pilfered goods back down the line to those who had already been searched. Our little squad could see this action and we had no intention of telling the Snowdrops anything.

Watching this show from within these uneven ranks one day, I noticed the approach of our sole army officer.

This five-foot-tall figure had Bonapartic leanings and was aptly nicknamed *The Boy Soldier*. He was a rather pretty blonde lad who lorded over a squad of six army signal core men. Their job being the repair and installation of telephone systems, as for some reason, the RAF did not install this form of telecommunications. He always behaved as though this modest command was a regiment of the *Grand Arme* about to launch a campaign. Looking like a refugee from a toy factory he strutted up and down our little platoon, his choir boy face vainly attempting to emulate the brisk expression so oft employed by John Mills in movies like *Ice Cold In Alex*.

Two well-polished little brown boots paused in front of me. Peering up at my wooden faced five-foot-six-inch height he queried.

"Have you shaved today Airman?"

I looked down at his peach-like cheeks that had obviously never been ravaged by anything sharper than a bath sponge and replied truthfully but probably foolishly.

"No sir. I don't shave yet."

How he kept a straight face whilst he ordered my name to be taken says a lot for the officer training of the UK because he carried it off without a flicker of those baby blue eyes.

With all due pomp and ceremony, I was hauled up before my section CO to answer this lack of personal hygiene. The forces delight on these occasions in practicing extreme melodrama calling the accused, 'Prisoner' and giving the suspect an escort of two of his work mates. Called from his kingdom next door, *The Boy Soldier* stamped in and gave evidence as though reporting the success of the D Day landings at Normandy as the allies invaded France in World War II. He then crashed back out to the obvious relief of the CO, quiet now being restored.

My CO was a fairly amiable man who, as long as communication with the outside world remained more or less unbroken, seemed quite happy to leave the running of things to us.

If this tranquillity was threatened by overzealous disciplinarians he had on occasion defended us and pulled rank on our persecutors. He looked up with weary resignation and said, "Well Freeman why didn't you shave?"

I then explained that having no beard yet I, therefore, had no reason to indulge the habit.

He had of course to give a stock reply.

"But if you're going on parade you're supposed to shave."

We were now in catch twenty-two country, that paradoxical land of military checkmate which means you are always in the wrong. To try and escape this I took a big chance.

"Sir, do I look unshaven today?"

"Not particularly."

"Well, I still haven't shaved."

Like that dying breed called gentlemen, this man had a sense of justice. *The Boy Soldier* was asked back in to shatter the calm once more with his reverberating boots. I was given a severe warning never to do this again, but no punishment was inflicted and that was the end of the matter as far as I was concerned. I suspect *The Boy Soldier* was given the hint to "Leave our chaps alone and stick to your own brown jobs in future."

As a footnote to this I would like to admit to an act of wanton defiance that I carried out after my last bomb dump guard. As the Land Rover bounced its way back to the camp, with a feeling of utter relief and happiness I threw my webbing belt as far across the passing desert as possible. It probably lies there still, a mute witness to a more peaceful era of Libya's history.

Chapter Twenty-One
The Chitty Box

During our enforced sojourn, time did have a tendency to hang heavily on our minds and, to distract ourselves, we would indulge in childish and sometimes rather cruel pranks.

An example of this was the case (pun intended) of Dave Stoneman's 'chitty' box. As everything in the armed services requires recognition in the form of a paper slip or 'chit' our deep-sea luggage was no exception. These boxes, which were used to mail our bulkier personal belongings home a few weeks prior to our departure, were waited for with a longing akin to the marooned *Treasure Island* character Benn Gunn's craving for that piece of cheese. This expectant time was known as 'sweating on your chitty box'.

Dave Stoneman was one of the more materialistically inclined of my cell mates. A constant customer at the duty-free shop he made numerous and possibly ostentatious purchases, delighting in parading this never-ending flow of cameras, table lamps, watches, electric shavers and radios all displayed around his bed space for us all to see and hopefully envy.

Although fairly innocuous, this competitive urge to keep up with the Joneses began to rankle in the closely confined atmosphere of the barrack room. It has to be noted that we were of the breed that shared toothpaste or sexual reminiscences with equal social ease.

So the early morning buzz of Dave's electric razor became exaggerated into the volume of a chainsaw, his mildly pretentious array of photographic equipment the luxurious gear of David Bailey and his radio the transmitter for Radio Moscow. One of his most ambitious acquisitions was an electric guitar and amplifier. Fortunately, the amplifier was in kit form and, after his attempt to assemble it, it blew up. So we were spared his amplified stumbling as he learnt to play.

When our chitty boxes finally arrived, we painted them black, then daubed our home address on the top in white paint. Dave carefully packed his, lying the guitar on top, and then nailed down the lid and went back to work at the duty-free shop. He had been such a good customer that by now he actually worked there giving him even more purchasing power. Wearying of this constant war of one-upmanship the rest of us, especially Ray Dodds who had still a year to serve in Libya's desolate acres, wracked our brains for some way to dent the superiority of our commercially minded comrade.

"I know," said Ray. "I'll hammer a six-inch nail through the lid of his chitty box right through that damn guitar."

I admit, to my shame, that I suggested that if he did perpetuate this act of vandalism he should paint the head of the nail black to avoid detection. The dastardly dead, was carried out and would remain undiscovered until unpacked in Dear Old Blighty. None of us could witness this but some did express a sadistic wish to be a fly on the wall.

When the rebellious activities of the current younger generation are being particularly frowned upon by their disapproving elders, the most well-worn cliché of the proposed cure to their lack of responsibility is, "Bring back National Service".

The supposed theory being that it will magically make men out of them, give them a sense of discipline and other such senile hyperbole. We were all volunteers, yet our discipline was more in the tradition of Richmal Crompton's characters of the *William* books than the stern upright maturity of such fantasised ideals. As for a responsible attitude, we all knew the real sin and that was getting caught. I suspect the current military generation's behaviour probably outdoes ours.

The eve of departure finally dawned and, coincidentally, a contingent of forces entertainers led by Edna Savage were to appear the same evening. The whole entertainment was billed as a dance followed by cabaret.

Part of the entourage were female harmony vocalists for the star's performance and I was lucky enough to persuade one of them to dance. Full of a final abandonment due to my imminent departure, I flung the kindly cooperative girl around the floor in a wild jive. Whilst attempting a rather ambitious gyration, my Sloppy Joe jumper caught in the zip of the back of her dress. Not realising this entanglement, I tried to spin her around, trail her arm over my shoulder and catch her hand at the end of the manoeuvre. Of course, this led to us becoming more firmly roped together and brought our dance to an abrupt and embarrassing halt.

The only possible method of extrication was to unzip her dress to her waist, exposing an enticing slice of female form and free my arm to the accompaniment of cries of, "C'mon Freeman you could have held out one more day".

Although this was of an ego deflating nature it seemed to be an ironically appropriate incident to finalize the past two futile years.

I boarded the homebound Comet 4c the next day unabashed and with high hopes of more fruitful encounters with the opposite sex.

Leaving anywhere is sad even a hellhole like El Adem. In its case, it being the people left behind that would be missed. So, amidst the joyous rapture as the plane took off, I did experience the odd twinge of regret for those whose company I would miss.

Happily, I was to meet most of them again but that is another story.